MEMOIR

REASONS WHY I LEFT THE AMISH COMMUNITY

BY SAM MILLER

DORRANCE
PUBLISHING CO
EST. 1920
PITTSBURGH, PENNSYLVANIA 15238

Dorrance Publishing Co
585 Alpha Drive
Pittsburgh, PA 15238
Visit our website at *www.dorrancebookstore.com*

ISBN: 978-1-6393-7310-9
eISBN: 978-1-6393-7707-7

MEMOIR

REASONS WHY I LEFT the AMISH COMMUNITY

CHAPTER ONE
LEAVING THE COMMUNITY

O N JUNE 4, 2009, it was a very beautiful day out. I was
working at home on my family farm. I was 17, at a point in my
life where I had to make a decision about what it was that I wanted to
do in life. I was brought up in an Amish community. The decision was
whether I wanted to stay Amish or if I wanted to leave the community.
It had been on my mind for some time. Leaving the community was
not the easiest thing to do. It just so happened that on this day, my
parents and some of my siblings were not at home. I thought to myself
this would be a great time to leave, since my parents were not at home;
it would be an easy way out for me.

My family were members of the Swartzentruber Amish, which is one
of the strictest Amish religions out there. If my parents would have been
home, it would have made it much harder for me to leave. Some of my
younger siblings had been home with my sister Mary. Mary was a couple
years older than me. I would have felt bad if I was the oldest one at home
and left my younger siblings at home by themselves. Being that my sister
Mary was older than me, I didn't feel quite as bad for leaving as I would
have if she was not there. However, I still felt bad for leaving. I knew it
would be a very long time till I would get to see them again.

As we gathered together that night for dinner, it was a sad moment
for me, knowing this would be the last meal with my family for a long

time. I did not know when the next time would be that I would get to sit at a table with my family for a meal.

I waited until everyone had gone to bed and were sleeping. Me and my older brother Dan were sharing a room together. Dan had also gone away with my parents, so I had the room all to myself. That made it even easier for me to leave. We would usually go to bed around 8:00.

I waited until around 10:00 that night, as I figured everyone would be asleep by then. I had chosen to leave at night, I didn't want anyone to see me leave or to wonder where I was going. I was very quiet leaving the house. I didn't want anyone to hear me. No one knew that I was planning on leaving. There had been a chair in the hallway. I pulled the chair out next to the stairway and left a note on the chair. I didn't leave much of a note. I don't remember the exact words that I wrote. It was something on the line of, "I have decided to leave the Amish community." I remember the note had been very short as I didn't know what else to write. All I left with was just the clothes that I was wearing, and out the door I went.

ONE YEAR EARLIER

Me and my brother Ura went for a walk out through the woods. We went for a joy walk, which was something we occasionally did. We came across an old bicycle. We were not allowed to have bicycles, but that was not going to stop me and Ura from trying it out. Neither of us had used a bicycle before this. However, we were both very interested in trying it out. Neither one of us could ride the bike. I had decided that I wanted to be able to ride the bike, and I was going to do whatever it took to be able to ride the bike. As for Ura, I don't know how much he actually rode the bike. For me, I had decided the only way I would ever learn how to ride the bike would be to do a lot of practice.

After doing enough practice, I was able to ride the bike. It was not easy. There were several times where I thought that I would never be able to ride the bike. I had never gotten really good, just good enough to say I can ride a bicycle.

So when the night came that I was leaving, as soon as I closed the house door, I took off running, out behind the barn and into the woods to go get the bike.

There had been this older gentleman named Carl; he would come to the farm quite often. I had decided I was going to his place and asked him if I could stay with him. He had lived around 17 miles from my parents' place, and for me, I didn't think I could walk 17 miles before it got daylight or someone would see me. I had never walked that far before, so I had no idea how long it would take. I just imagine it would take a really long time. This is why I had chosen to use the bicycle as I thought I could get there a lot faster.

I also had no idea how scary it was going to be running away in the middle of the night. I heard many dogs barking. It seemed almost every house I went by had a dog barking. I had no idea so many people had dogs. It didn't really bother me hearing all the dogs bark other than for this one house I went by. I believe they had two pit bulls out in front of the house; their house had sat up on top of a hill. By that time, I was very tired. So instead of pedaling the bike up the hill, I decided to push the bike up the hill to give my legs a little rest. When I got right in front of their house, both dogs came running out barking at the top of their lungs. I got on the bike and started pedaling as fast as I could. Both dogs chased me down the road a ways, but after a while, they turned around when back home. What a relief that was. I kept going down the road. It wasn't long until I came to where there was a wooded area on both sides of the road for quite a while.

All of the sudden, I heard a pack of coyote hollering. The coyote had seemed close by. However, they were not close enough to really bother me. Being that I had a bicycle, I felt safe. I had taken mostly all back roads, as I didn't want to be going down the main road and have someone see me. Plus, my bicycle didn't have light nor did it have any brakes. Whenever I came to a hill where it was a pretty good downhill slope, I would walk the bike down the hill. As I was worried that I may go too fast down the hill and end up having an accident.

It was around 2:00 to 3:00 in the morning when I got to Carl's house. Right before I got to his house there was a small section of woods where I parked the bicycle. I thought it would be a great place to hide it, so no one would see it. I started walking toward the house. My plan was to knock on the door. As I almost got to the house, something told me knocking on the door was not going to be a good idea. So I stopped for a minute to figure out what could be my next plan.

There were a couple older barns that he had at his place. One of them had been out behind his house, which was a smaller barn. There was a bigger barn to the right of the house. I decided to walk in the bigger barn. At this time, I was just looking for a place where I could lay down and get some sleep for the rest of the night. The barn was completely empty. The only thing for me to lay on in the barn would have been the concrete floor. At this point of time, I had started feeling hopeless that I would find a place to sleep. I started walking down through the barn. I saw a couple of windows in the back of the barn. I decided to look out the window to see if I see anything out behind the barn. As I looked out the window, I saw an old car sitting out behind the barn.

I thought maybe that would be a good place to sleep. So I walked out behind the barn to the car. At first I looked through the window to see if there was anything in the car. The car seemed to be pretty much empty. I opened the back door as I thought sleeping in the back seat would be a good idea. When I opened the back door, I realized the car had a somewhat bad smell. However, I was very tired. Sleeping in the back of this old car seemed like it was my only option. So that is what I ended up doing. It didn't take me long to fall asleep. I actually slept very well.

When I woke up, the sun was shining through the window. I sat in the car for a while, and I started thinking, *What if Carl is not going to let me stay at his place?* I really didn't have a plan B. All I knew was that I didn't want to go back home. I thought, *There is only one way to find out if he will let me stay at his place for the time being.*

I went to the house and knocked on the door. Carl just yelled out and said, "Come on in," not even knowing who it was. I opened the door and walked into the house. He seemed to be a bit surprised to see who it was. Meanwhile, I was very nervous as I didn't know what to expect. Carl had a deep voice, more of a loud spoken person.

He asked me, "What it is that I can help you with?"

I told him that, "I want to leave the Amish and was wondering if I could stay here for a while or for the time being."

He just looked at me for a few seconds. Then asked me, "Do you want to leave the Amish community?"

I replied, "Yes, I do."

He just thought for a moment then told me if I wanted to leave the community, I would be welcome to stay at his house as long as I want to. What a relief that was for me, knowing that I didn't have to go back home or come up with a different plan. We sat at his house and talked for a while. Finally, he said that he was going to town for several hours and would be back afterwards. By this time, I was getting really hungry but wasn't going to say anything to Carl as I felt that I asked for a lot as it was. After he went to town, I just hung out at his house. If I remember right, for the most part, I just sat on the couch watching TV, something I never got to do at home.

But as time went on, I kept getting hungrier and hungrier. Finally, I decided I was going to look in the fridge or freezer to see if he had any food that I could eat. I didn't like the idea of going through his fridge to find something to eat. I was worried that he may notice that food had gone missing and would get upset with me for eating food without asking him. I did end up finding food in his fridge that I did eat. I don't exactly remember what I ate.

It was around noon by the time he got back. When he got back, he asked me how I was doing or if there was anything I would like to do. I said that I was doing good. I also said, "If you have time, I would like to go get a haircut somewhere."

He asked me if I was sure that I wanted to get a haircut. He thought maybe I would want some more time to think about it. I told him that I was ready to get a haircut as I had been thinking about this day for quite some time now. So he called the place where he went to get his haircut. After he got off the phone, he said that he had made an appointment for later that afternoon.

My hair was pretty long. Our hair had to be long enough to where the bottom of our ear would not show.

When we arrived at the place to get a haircut, I started getting very nervous, as this was going to be the first time in my life to get a haircut from someone other than my mom. Any time we needed a haircut, our mother would always give us a haircut. We walked into the place where we had to wait for a little while as they were busy giving other people haircuts. It wasn't long until the lady called my name. My face had gotten very red, and my heart was beating very fast. As I sat in the chair, the lady asked me how I was doing and also how short I wanted to get my haircut. I replied saying that I was doing good. As I'm not sure how short I told her I wanted to have my haircut. All I remember was that I had gotten it cut really short.

As I was sitting in the chair, the lady was cutting my hair. My heart just kept pounding really fast. I had also been facing a big mirror. However, I just kept looking at the floor thinking to myself that pretty much the whole Amish community would look down on me for what I was doing. Growing up, we were taught if we were to leave the community that God would never forgive us for what we had done. When the time came that we passed away, we would not make it into heaven. Instead of making it into heaven, God would create a very hot fire, and our body would be burned. I had also believed this would happen to me if I ever left the community. This was one of the reasons why my heart was pounding so fast while I was sitting in the chair getting my hair cut. I had also been thinking about all the people that I was letting down for leaving. (Especially my family.)

After the lady got done giving my haircut, she asked me if I liked the looks of it. Meanwhile, I hadn't taken my eyes off the floor. But the time had come for me to take my eyes off the floor and look in the mirror. So I did, and I told the lady that it looked really good. There was part of me that did feal really good about the haircut. But the other part of me kept thinking about how disappointed my family must be at me, as well as the rest of the Amish community.

After we left the haircut place, on our way home, Carl decided to stop by the grocery store to pick up some groceries. I also wanted to get groceries, but I didn't have any money, and I didn't want to ask Carl for money as I felt that he had already done plenty for me. I certainly didn't want Carl to feel like I was taking advantage of him.

As we were going through the grocery store, he told me to feel free to get whatever it was I would like. I told Carl that there wasn't really anything that I wanted. I didn't want to tell him the real reason why I was not picking some groceries off the shelf for myself. He finally looked at me and said, "If you are not getting groceries because you don't have any money, not to worry." Carl told me he would pay for the groceries. By this time, I had felt grateful that I had chosen to go to his place as I could tell he was willing to help me out with whatever it is that I needed. Carl was the kind of person who was very much stuck in his own ways. In other words, you could say he was a little on the hard headed side. However, deep inside, he had a big heart and would nearly give the shirt off his back to help someone out.

I didn't end up staying at his place for very long, only for about a week. One of the first things I told him was that I wanted to get a job.

He asked what it is that I would like to do for work. At the time, I didn't really care what I did for work. I just wanted to make enough money to support myself. Doing carpentry work was what I was best at and was what I really wanted to do. Growing up, working with wood was what we mostly did. So I felt very confident about myself that I would be good at doing carpentry work and could do a great job. But unfortunately, Carl didn't really know of a carpentry company that I could work for.

He did have a friend who was working in construction. His name is Timmy. A lot of the work that they were doing at the time was landscaping, and they were looking for someone to work for them. I wasn't very familiar with that type of work, but I needed a job as I thought this would be a great opportunity until I found a carpentry company to work for. It was less than a week after I left the community. I started working for the construction company. I was very excited knowing that I had a job and was going to be able to earn some money.

In the Amish community, we have to work for our parents until we were the age of 21. Up until the age of 21, any money we earn has to go to our parents, so earning money was something I never got to do, not that I could keep for myself. All 17 years of my life, I never got to have money in my pocket that I was mine. I had always wanted the feeling of having money in my pocket that I could say was mine. That's why earning money for me was something I was very excited about.

It wasn't until sometime after I had realized how lucky I was to be able to get a job in construction. I didn't have a social security number nor did I have a birth certificate. The only way for me to make money at the time was to work under the table. I also didn't have a driver's license, so going to work or anywhere else, I always had to ask for a ride. Luckily for me, working with Timmy, he was willing to come pick me up and bring me back home.

After several days of working with him and coming to pick me up, he offered me to stay at his place. He said they had an extra bedroom that was not being used at the time. He told me I was more than welcome to stay with them. It would also save him from having to drive to Carl's house to pick me up. Since I was working with him, I thought this would be the best idea to stay with Timmy and his family. The one thing that always stuck to me was whenever I went to live with someone, I was always worried they may think that I'm taking advantage of them. But for me, it was not like I could get a place on my own. Living with someone else was pretty much the only choice I had.

As time went on, waking up in the morning and eating breakfast and going to work, I would often think of my family, especially my mother, as I can imagine it had to be pretty hard on her. The first couple of weeks were hard for me as I would think of home a lot, thinking of all the people I had let down. After several months, I started to get used to living English life, and I was getting used to living away from my family more and more each day. However, living English life came to an end really fast for me. One day we were at work, Timmy got a phone call from the police station, and they were looking for me. My father had gone to the police station and told them what had happened. He also asked them to bring me back home. Since I wasn't the age of 18, I didn't have any other choice other than having to go back home until I was the age of 18.

I started thinking about what I could do to avoid having to go back home. One of the first things that came to me was that I could possibly run away and hide myself where no one could find me. However, I was told if I was to do so, they would end up putting a search warrant out for me. By this time, I had realized there was no other way; having to go home was my only option. Just as I had started feeling like my life was coming together, I had to go back home, which was the last thing I wanted to do.

After Timmy got done talking to the police, he told me the situation. There was going to be a policeman at the construction company shop the following day at 5:00 in the evening to bring me back home. That was also around the time we would get back to the shop from working for the day. For the rest of the day and the whole next day, I was very upset by the fact that I had to go back home. The next morning came around and I got up just like any other day, ate breakfast, and went to work. I remember I barely spoke a word that day. At the end of the day as we were on our way back to the company shop, I was sitting in the back seat, and we had several other people riding with us. We had a one-hour ride back to the shop. On our way back, I looked pretty well out the window the whole way back. I felt very depressed. I had made a couple friends I was enjoying hanging out with.

CHAPTER 2
HAVING TO RETURN TO THE COMMUNITY UNTIL OF AGE

WHEN WE ARRIVED BACK AT THE SHOP, the policeman wasn't there yet, but it wasn't long afterwards he showed up. He visited with Timmy and some of the other guys in the shop before we left. After he got done visiting with them, he looked at me and said, "I think it is time we leave."

As we walked toward the police car, I thought he was going to put handcuffs on and make me sit in the backseat. I had always thought this was the only way they were allowed to have someone ride in their car in a situation like this. When we got to the car, he asked me if I had a pocket knife on me or any other weapon on me, or if I was going to hurt him in any way. I replied saying that I didn't have any weapon on me nor was I planning on hurting him. I was actually scared of him. We were taught the policemen are nobody you want to mess around with. After I got done replying to his questions, he told me I could sit in the front seat. He did mention that he's technically not supposed to let me sit in the front seat. However, he didn't want to bring me home in handcuffs in front of my family, which I was glad for. Being brought home in a police car in front of my family was bad enough. On our way to my parents' place, he tried having several different conversations, but in a situation like this, I was very quiet. Not because I didn't want to talk; it was just the way we were brought up. In the Amish, we are not nearly as open to carry on a conversation as the outside world is.

The policeman asked me if I was planning on leaving again. I said no, that I was not planning on leaving again. I however had planned on leaving again. I was afraid if I was to tell him any differently, as he would tell my parents. I did not want my parents to know that I was planning on leaving again. If I would have told my father that I was planning on leaving again, he would have gotten very upset with me. My father had a very bad temper. He was not afraid to scream and yell at me and my siblings. There were many times he would even take it further than that. For me, I knew I could never tell my family or anyone around me that I had plans on leaving the first time and the second time. If my father would have ever found out, it would not have been a good day for me.

When we arrived at my parents' house, my father came walking out of the house. I got out of the car, and my father looked at me for a second then told me I should go to the house, so I did. I could tell he hadn't changed a bit. I went into the house and sat on a chair by the table. My father stayed outside talking to the policeman for a while. My mother came walking into the kitchen where I was sitting. She asked me several questions. The only questions I remember my mother asking me was if I wanted to put on my Amish clothes. I knew I had no other choice than having to put on my Amish clothes. So I said, "Yes, I do." After I put on my Amish clothes, I went back to the kitchen and sat on the same chair I was sitting in before. I had no idea what I was supposed to do or if I was getting some kind of punishment.

After my father got done talking to the policeman, I never did find out what they talked about. He came back to the house, and he went and got my mom. They both came into the kitchen where I was still sitting. My father asked me to follow them into the living room. After we walked into the living room, my father shut the door behind us. When I saw that he shut the door, I had started to get worried that my father was going to punish me. Getting punished in the Amish most of the time would lead to getting a butt spanking, which was what I thought my father was going to give me. My father's butt spanking would at times be very severe. He had a leather belt in his dresser drawer, and he was not afraid to use it. Most of the time when we were in trouble or had done something to upset my father, he would ask us to come into the living room and shut the door and give us a spanking.

My father had decided not to give me a spanking. But some of the things he told me were not much better. My father asked me why I left and if I had plans on leaving again. I knew there was no way I could tell my father the truth, so I lied to him, just so I wouldn't get in more trouble than I had already been in. My father told me, God and the Amish community would never forgive me for what I did. He also said I would never make it to heaven. Instead, God would create a very hot fire and my body would be burn.

After my father told me that, I thought to myself, *Why would I want to stay in a community where they think what I have done is so bad and cannot forgive me for what I have done? They will always look down on me for what I had done.* As I thought that to myself, I also thought, *This is no way I want to live my life.*

My eighteenth birthday was two months away. I thought I would make the best of it until I turned 18. In the Amish community, we would only go to church every two weeks. It just so happened the week I was brought back, we had to go to the church that Sunday. I didn't want to go to church. I knew people would look down on me for what I had done. However, in the Amish community, you didn't get to choose if you wanted to go to church; if you were feeling good and not sick, you had to go to church.

After church in the evening, we would have an evening singing. The evening singing was for those who were older than 17 but not married. Once you got married, you would not go to the evening singing anymore. When you turned the age of 17, you were allowed to go out "rumspringa," meaning you were allowed to go out on Saturday nights to go on dates. We were only allowed to go out on dates Saturday nights or Sundays nights after evening singing.

Dating in the Amish is very different from the English world. If there was a girl you really liked and wanted to have a date with, it may not always work in your favor. You don't get to go ask the girl yourself if she wants to have a date with you.

On Saturday night, all the guys who are old enough to be rumspringa and didn't have a girlfriend would all get together. For the women, they were not allowed to go out on Saturday nights. They were only allowed to go out Sunday nights to the evening singing. As all the guys would gather together Saturday evening. Sometimes we would just gossip, but most of the Saturday eves, we would try to take someone on a date. If I was taken on a date, all the other guys would get together and decide who they would want me to have a date with. Then they would come to me and ask me if I wanted to have a date with that girl. If I decide I don't want to have a date with her, I can say no. But if I wanted to have a date with her, I would say yes. If I agreed to have a date, we would all go to the girl's house. Some of the guys would go into the house and go upstairs into the girl's rooms and wake her up. For the rest of us, we would stay outside. After they woke the girl up, they would ask her if she wanted to have a date with me. If she wanted to have a date with me, she would say yes; if not, she would say no.

It wasn't always as easy as saying no if you didn't want to have a date with the girl. A lot of the times, the guys would push you until you would say yes, and it was the same for the girl.

But if the girl did agree to have a date with you, the guys who had gone in the house would come back out to get the rest of us boys, and we would all go upstairs in the girl's room. We would all sit around and talk for a while, then the rest of the guys would leave, and me and the girl would be all alone in the room. We would stay up for a while. After visiting for a while, we would shut off the lights and lay in bed with each other.

We also had to give each other at least one hug and one kiss, otherwise it was not considered a date. (If you are an outsider, you may think this is all very confusing and weird…) When it was time for me to go home, if I liked the girl, before I left the room, I would ask her if she would want to have a date again. If she said yes, we would continue dating, and we would now be considered boyfriend and girlfriend. Once we were considered a couple, we were only allowed to have a date every two weeks on Saturday night. The only other time we were allowed to see each other was Sunday evening after evening singing. I would be allowed to give her a ride home after the singing. Otherwise, we were not allowed to see each other until marriage. I did go on several dates but never had a girlfriend.

After I went back during the two months' time I was only allowed to go to the evening singing one time. For the rest of the time, other than going to church, I had to stay home. This was part of the punishment for what I had done. It didn't bother me that I was not able to go to the evening singing. I knew at the time I was not going to fit in or be able to enjoy my life.

For me, I was enjoying being home with my family more than I would have if I went to the evening singing or if I went out on Saturday evening. It felt good being home with my family, getting to sit at the same table to eat dinner and sleep under the same roof as the rest of my family. I knew when I turned 18, I was leaving again. So the more time I got to spend with my family, the better it was for me. This time around when I was leaving, just like the first time, I had no idea when the next time I would be that I'd get to sit at the same table to eat dinner as the rest of my family.

Before I had left the second time, I thought it could be a couple years before I got to sit at the same table to eat dinner as the rest of my family. However, 10 years have gone by, and I still haven't got to sit at the same table to eat a meal with my family, nor have I got to go home to visit my family. As time went on, I thought of my family a lot. There are times where it brings tears to my eyes not being able to see my family and knowing my family doesn't support the lifestyle I have chosen to live.

Before I left the first time, I had never wanted to leave the community. Growing up, I had always wanted to follow the religion because I thought that was the right thing to do. However, at the time, my father had made it very hard for me to be able to fit in and enjoy the lifestyle.

My father is the bishop in our community. He was very strict and wanted me and my siblings to be better than everyone else as far as following the religion. This is how I felt. He didn't want us to show off or be cool. He wanted us to walk a straight line. As we all know, when you cannot have the same amount of fun and be as cool as your friends are, you are usually the one who gets picked on, which is just what had started happening to me.

As we are growing up, we all get excited to turn at 17 years old. We get to go out on Saturday night and hang out with all the guys who are of age. It makes you feel like you are cool. This is how I felt for the first couple of months after I turned 17; I was really enjoying my life. But after that, it all started going downhill. We had to wear suspenders. As far as I know all Amish children wear suspenders until they get to a certain age where their parents allow them to go without them. For some of the Amish, they would allow their boys to go without them when they are done going to school, which is the age of 14. For others, they would allow their boys to go without them when they turn the age of 17.

My father had decided he wanted me and my brother to wear suspenders until we were the age of 21, which became an issue for me. As I was the only teenager at the time, about the age of 17 that had to wear suspenders, it never really bother me until one of the other boys my age asked me why I wear suspenders. I told him my father wouldn't allow me to go without them until the age of 21. This is when it started to bother me. But several days went by. I thought to myself and had decided I wasn't going to let it get to me and go on with life.

It wasn't long until it happened again. This time, when it got brought up it was more like they were making fun of me for having to wear suspenders. As one of the guys had said something about me wearing suspenders, and everyone else just laughed at me because I had to wear suspenders.

This time, it really bothered me a lot. The more I thought about it, the more it bothered me. I started thinking of what it is that I could do. I thought about asking my father if it would be okay if I went without suspenders since all the other guys my age didn't have to wear them. All I wanted was to be able to fit in and enjoy my life.

I knew my father wouldn't let me go without them. He had his mind very well set on that we had to wear suspenders until the age of 21. So I thought, *What else can I do?* The only thing that came to my mind was to stay home and avoid going out on Saturday nights hanging out with all the guys. Staying home, I had known it was going to bother me, but not as much as going out and getting made fun of for what I had to wear. So staying home is what I started doing as much as I could. It came to the point where it didn't bother me staying home.

Several months went by where I pretty well just stayed at home. After that, I started to go out on Saturday nights again. It was only because of our neighbor's son John. John was close to my age. As one Saturday night, he stopped by our place and asked me if I would want to go out with him and some of the other guys. I thought for a moment and decided that it was a while since I had gone out. So I ended up going out and hanging out with him and the guys. At the time, I did enjoy hanging out with John. He was never the type to judge someone for what they had to wear.

It wasn't long after John decided he wanted to take me on a date. All by himself. At first, I didn't want to go on a date, as I liked the way things was going. I had also thought it wouldn't be the right time. But

John kept pushing me until I said I would only go on a date if he would promise me that he would not tell anyone. John promised me that he wouldn't tell anyone; he had gone as far as guaranteeing me that he wouldn't tell anyone.

In the Amish community, the word guarantee is a word that is rarely used. It is only used if you are sure that you can keep your promise. So when John guaranteed me that he wouldn't tell anyone, I didn't think twice. I thought I could trust him. Being taken on a date in the Amish, we would always keep it a secret and not tell anyone. I don't know why it was supposed to be such a big secret. My thought is that is the way it's always been. So when the Saturday night came that he had planned to take me on a date, he came to my place. He came to the house and came upstairs to the room where I was. I was pretty well ready to go. We sat there talking for a while.

When we got done talking, we went out to the barn. I had to get one of the horses ready and hitch it to the buggy. John had helped me get the horse ready and get it hitched to the buggy. After we got all done hitching the horse to the buggy, we were all ready to go. John had his own buggy. Since he was taking me on a date, he was going home long before me. So riding together wasn't going to work out.

The date went well. This was not the first time I had gone on a date. The first time I had a date, I had no idea what I was supposed to do or how a date went. Nobody tells you what to do when you're on your first date. I had asked my sister Mary a couple times, but she wouldn't tell me. All she said was, "You'll have to wait and find out for yourself."

For the guys when they go on their first date, the girl is supposed to lead. Meaning she is the one who will put her arms around you and give you a hug and kiss. After the guy's first date, they are supposed to lead from there on.

When John took me on a date, I knew what to do. The first time around, I didn't even know what time I was supposed to get up and go home. I just finally decided to get up and go home, not even knowing if that was what I was supposed to do. As time went on, I found out that I did get up and went home around the time I was supposed to. However, my friendship with John went downhill very fast after the date. It turns out John did not stick to his word. John turned out to be what I would call a liar. Three or four days later, I found out that just about everyone in the community had already found out that I had a date.

The first person who said something to me was my brother Dan. Dan was dating a girl named Katie, and as time went on, he got married to her. Katie found out that I had a date. She wrote Dan a letter and sent it in the mail. Dan received the letter the same day.

The Amish community is not allowed to have a phone. The only way to get a message to someone is to write a letter or go to their house. Katie decided to write Dan a letter. We lived about three miles from Katie's family. The mail lady would go by Katie's place before she would go past our place. Katie wrote on the outside of the envelope: *Importing mail please drop off today*, which is just what the mail lady did. When we got done eating lunch, one of us would go out and get the mail. It just so happened our parents were not at home that day. When I or one of my siblings would go get the mail, we would always bring the mail into the house and hand it to our father. Being that our parents were not at home and Dan was the oldest one at home, he decided to look through the mail before he went outside to work. I had already left the house and was out in the barn getting the horses ready to go out and do field work.

Just as I was getting ready to head to the field, here comes Dan walking down through the barn at a pretty fast pace. He came up to me and all he said to me was, "You're pretty dumb for trusting John." I kept doing what I was doing. I never said a word to Dan as I was very surprised that John had already told other people that he took me on a date and who I had a date with.

As I went out in the field to do field work that afternoon, I was very upset that John had told anyone, and that he had lied to me. In most situations, after several days, I would move on with life and not let it bother me. But it just so happened that we had to go to church the next Sunday coming up. I knew pretty much everyone would have found out by Sunday.

This was one Sunday I wished I could fake being sick and wouldn't have to go to church. Me trying to fake something…I was not very good at it. I knew someone was going to bring it up. I also had a feeling that I was going to be made fun of for who I had a date with.

When Sunday came around, we all went to church. Church went very well; no one said anything to me until the evening singing, and just like I thought I got laughed at and made fun of for who I had a date with. After I got home that night, I was lying in bed with tears in my eyes. All I had wanted was to be able to fit in. John was one of the few friends I had left, and now he turned his back on me. At this point, I knew I was not going to fit in or be able to enjoy my life in the Amish community.

As the night went on, I finally ended up falling asleep. For the next couple of days, I was really depressed. I knew I had to come up with a different plan in order for me to be able to enjoy my life, and the only thing that came to my mind was to leave the community. After several weeks of thinking about leaving the community, I finally made up my mind that I was going to leave the community and would never be going on a Amish date again. It was certainly a very hard time for me, not being able to fit in and enjoy my life.

I didn't really have a date. I wanted to leave just when the time was right. I had decided to live the Amish life until that day came. The day came much sooner than I thought it was going to. All the guys that were out rumspringa and had made plans to gather together to have a small fire and roasted hotdogs. It was named the "Hotdog Roasting Party."

The gathering was going to be the following Saturday evening. Some of us guys were supposed to bring bread, and the rest of the guys were going to bring the hotdogs. The bread was supposed to be store-bought bread. The reason the bread was supposed to be from a store was because we rarely had store bought bread and it would make us feel "cooler." As we all know, buying bread and hotdogs does not cost a lot of money.

I didn't have any money, not even one cent, and I could not help pay for anything. I knew if I went and didn't have any money to help pay for anything, I would feel guilty being there, eating someone else's food that I did not help pay for. But at the same time, by me not going, all the guys were going to question me as to why I didn't show up, and if our elders ever found out about it, I was going to be the one getting the blame for it because I was the only one not there. Having a party of any kind is very against the Amish religion.

I'm not exactly sure who came up with the idea of having a fire and roasting hotdogs. Whoever it was had been planning it for about a month as they wanted to be sure all the guys that were out rumspringa were going to show up. As the time got closer, I started to realize that a lot of people knew about the hotdog roosting party, and I knew only more people were going to find out. I had also known if I went and sat next to a fire, my cloth would smell like smoke. My mother had a very sharp noise. I knew she would smell the smoke on the cloth and would want to know where I had gone.

About a week before the Hotdog Roasting Party, I made up my mind I was not going to the party. With all the people who had known about the Hotdog Roasting Party, I knew somebody was not going to be able to keep the secret. But me not going was not exactly keeping me from getting in trouble. My father would still punish me for knowing about it and not telling him. But if I would have told my parents, the rest of the community was going to find out for all the guys that were rumspringa would never want to hang out with me ever again.

I had decided I was going to take a punishment over losing all my friends. At the time, I didn't really feel like I had any friends. but I just didn't want to make things worse than they had already been. The worst part of being punished by my father is most likely he was going to give me a bigger punishment than the rest of the guys would have got. My father would have felt giving me a bigger punishment than the other parents in the community would make him look better. My father had this saying, "If you know that someone is doing something they are not supposed to do and you don't tell anyone, you are just as bad as they are." In the Amish community, being stricter than everyone else makes you feel like you are doing a better job following the religion, which is just what my father wanted to do. He wanted to follow the religion better than anybody else in the community.

However my father, being very strict and thinking he was doing a better job following the religion or thinking it would make him look better than everyone else for the most part, was not necessarily doing a better job following the religion. By punishing us over every little thing, it may have made him feel like he was doing a better job following the religion. But at the end of the day, he was not doing a better job. The only thing it did for me was make me realize I wanted to be around him as little as possible. My father was not the only one very strict; there were several other men in our community who acted very strictly and rarely smiled; they would always walk around with a very angry-looking face. In our community, from what I saw, my father had the strictest rules, which was just the way he wanted it to be. Growing up having a father who was very strict and angry made it very hard for me to fit in and enjoy the Amish life.

As the days went by, I kept looking for an opportunity to leave the community. It just so happened during the time my parents was gone, Carl stopped by our house to visit. I was out in front of the barn when he drove in. It was right after we got done eating lunch. Carl drove right up to the barn where I was. None of my other siblings were next to me.

Me and Carl started visiting, and he had asked me if my parents were home. I told him they had not been home and were not going to be for several days. I asked Carl if I could come visit him during the time my parents were gone. I didn't tell him that I wanted to leave the community. Carl told me I could come visit any time I wanted to. I don't think Carl actually thought I was coming to visit him, as I think this is why he was so surprised to see me when I did show up at his house.

After Carl left, I decided that night I was going to leave the community. This was the first time I knew when I was leaving the community, I saw a good opportunity to leave. So I decided to do so. After I had left, I found out most of the Amish in the community were very surprised to hear that I left. Some of them didn't believe it when they first found out, which was not necessarily a surprise to me. I also found out the Hotdog Roasting Party never happened. Just like I thought, someone was not able to keep the secret and the elders found out about it. I was just glad that I was no longer there to get punished for something I didn't want to do in the first place. It felt great knowing I no longer had to live in a place and life where I always have to fear the next time I was going to get punished over something that didn't make any sense to get punished for.

We lived in Lawrenceville, New York. We moved to this area from Ohio in 2004. This was a new Amish community that had just started, and for five years nobody left the community until I did. This was one of the reasons the community was so surprised to hear that I left. But it was not the only reason they was surprised to hear that I left. For the most part, when you hear of someone leaving the Amish, it is usually someone who is more of a wild child. I was not a wild child at all. The Hotdog Roasting Party was certainly what put a lot of pressure on me to leave. I had left four days before the party was supposed to happen, and the day after I had left was when the word started to spread and the elders found out. How lucky I had felt to be able to get out in time.

CHAPTER 3

SECOND TIME LEAVING THE COMMUNITY

WHEN I LEFT THE SECOND TIME, I don't think that it was such a big surprise for the community to hear that I left. It is not unheard of for someone to leave the community and end up coming back home several months or within a year after they left, simply because they did not like living the English life. However, those who end up returning to the community before they are ready are most likely to leave again. This was just the case for me; I was not ready to go back home. I had wanted to experience the outside world more before I went home, and I also didn't want to go back home before I felt like I was going to fit in. I always thought if I was to return, it wouldn't be until the age of 21. After the age of 21, we don't have to follow our parents' rules anymore. We can pretty much do whatever it is we would like as long as we follow the religion, and this is why I thought the age of 21 would be the right age to return.

But after my father had told me how the Amish community would never forgive me for what I had done, I had decided I was not going to return to the community after I left the second time.

When I left the second time, it was much easier for me to leave than it was the first time around. Before I went back home, I had made a couple friends whose names were Matt and Austin. Matt and Austin would hang out with each other quite often. I had gotten to know Matt because he was working for the same company I was.

After a couple weeks of working with Matt, he offered to come hang out with him and Austin during the weekend, and for me, of course, I wanted to go hang out with them. This sounded like it was going to be a great time. Living in the Amish community, we were not allowed to drink alcohol. I had always wanted to have the feeling of drinking alcohol, which I got to do plenty of by hanging out with Matt and Austin. Matt was not much of an alcohol drinker; however, Austin was not afraid to do his fair share of drinking and partying, which is just what I wanted to do. We never got to do anything like this living in the community.

I would hang out with Matt and Austin whenever I was not working. When the day came that I had to go back, I told them to come pick me up after I turned 18. They told me they would come pick me up. The next couple of months went by, and I didn't see either one of them. I had honestly thought they moved on and pretty much forgot about me and wanted nothing to do with me. It made me sad thinking this could be true. We had a sawmill where we would cut logs into lumber and sell it to people in the community and also to people on the outside of the community. Most of our customers came from the outside.

It was two days before my birthday, me and my brother Joe were working at the sawmill. It was a very damp and rainy day. It was getting later in the afternoon. All of the sudden, here comes a black Toyota truck pulling in by the sawmill. The minute I saw the truck, I knew exactly who it was. It was Matt and Austin! I was very glad to see them. I was also very surprised to see them. They had come to pretend like they wanted to buy lumber. They were not interested in buying lumber at all; they had come to see me and wanted to know if I was going to leave the community again.

I was very lucky my father was not at the sawmill. If he would have been, I would've never got to talk to Matt and Austin. They wanted me to jump in the truck with them and leave. I told them I didn't want to leave in broad daylight. I wasn't even sure if I wanted to leave. I started thinking maybe I should wait to leave until several months after my birthday. However, I thought for a moment and decided now is a great opportunity to leave. But I had also decided I was not going to leave while it was daylight. I didn't want any of my family to see me leave. My thought was it would be best if I left in the middle of the night, where no one would see me. I thought it would be a lot harder on my family to see me leave in daylight than it was going to be if they woke up and noticed that I was no longer there. I told Matt and Austin that I wanted to wait until after my birthday. My birthday was on a Thursday. I told them to pick me up that Saturday night. Why had I chosen to have them pick me up on Saturday night? Since Saturday nights were when we would go out, I thought this would be a great time to leave as I could pretend like I was going out to hang out with the other boys.

This time around, my parents were home, so leaving the house was going to be a little bit more of a challenge. Once I left the house it, was going to be an easy way out. I certainly was not going to have to peddle a bicycle for 17 miles and sleep in an old car.

I had told Matt and Austin to pick me up at 10:00 that night, as this was about the same time I would have left to go out to meet up with the other boys. I was very worried that my father was going to hear me come down the stairs and would want to know where I was going.

We did have a bathroom that was attached to the house, but only the women would use the bathroom, and for us boys, we would go to the barn when we had to go to the bathroom. Sometimes we would just take a walk out in the woods to go to the bathroom, so I had a couple options if my father did see me leaving the house. Either I could tell him I was going to the bathroom or I could tell him I was going out to hang out with the other guys.

I was also worried my father would not let me go out to hang out with the other boys. When I went back, he had told me if I wanted to go anywhere, I would have to ask him first. I was not allowed to go anywhere without his permission, which made me very upset. None of the other boys my age had to ask their parents when they wanted to go out on Saturday night. It felt like every time my father got a chance, he would make it harder for me to enjoy the Amish life.

So I decided it would be best if my father was to see me leaving the house to just tell him I was going to use the bathroom.

Me and my brother Dan were sharing a room. Since Dan had a girlfriend, he was going to be leaving around 9:00 to go have a date with her. After he left, I had the room all to myself.

As I was laying in bed waiting for 10:00 to come, the closer it got to being 10:00, the faster my heart was beating. The last thing I wanted to happen was for my parents to see me leaving the house. We lived on top of a hill. I had told Matt and Austin to drive up the hill and go by our house, go up to the neighbor's house, and turn around and drive back by our house, then go to the bottom of the hill and wait for me there.

I started thinking, *What if they won't show up. How am I going to leave if they don't show up?* I decided if they were not coming to pick me up, I was not leaving that night.

It was about five minutes from 10:00. I could hear the black Toyota truck coming up the hill. The truck had a sound like no other truck around. Matt came to pick me up by himself. He did just what I had asked him to do. He went up to the neighbor's and turned around, went to the bottom of the hill, and waited for me.

This time around, I had decided not to leave a note. I did leave my suspender behind, and I also left my pocket watch behind. I had also left both of these behind the first time I left. I left both of the items on my bed, which is also just what I had done the first time I left. So I knew when my family would find the suspender and the watch, they would know I had left again.

The reasons for leaving the suspender and the watch behind: I didn't like that I had to wear suspenders when none of the other boys my age had to, so leaving the suspender behind was to give my parents a hint why I had left. For the watch, when we turned the age of 15, we would be allowed to carry a watch. The watch that my father gave us is a windup watch. We are not allowed to have a battery watch. It was against Amish religion to have battery watches. The watch our father gave us was not a cheap watch. If you took good care of the watch, it would last you for the rest of your life. When my father had handed me the watch, he told me if I ever came to the point where I didn't want to follow his rules or the Amish religion to give the watch back to him. Since my father had asked to give the watch back to him if I don't want to follow the religion, I thought leaving the watch behind would be the right thing to do.

After Matt had gone back by the house, I lay in bed for about 10 minutes longer till I got up and went downstairs. My mother and father had both been gone to bed. I hurried up, put on my pair of boots, and went out the door. As soon as I closed the door, I took off running down the road as fast as I could go. I ran down to the bottom of the hill where Matt was waiting for me.

Matt brought me back to Timmy's place where I was living before I went back to the community. Timmy's family had gone away for the night, but they were aware that I may be stopping by their place while they were gone. They left the door unlocked, so I could get in and get my English clothes. I walked into the bedroom where I was sleeping before. The room was still just the same as it was when I went back. Timmy's family had felt so confident that I was coming back to live with them, they went and bought some more clothes for me.

Since Timmy and his family were not at home, Matt asked me if I wanted to come spend the night at his place. I had decided since Timmy's family was not at home, I would go spend the night at Matt's place. It was about a 45-minute drive from Timmy's place to Matt's house. Matt was living with his mother at the time. Matt and his mother had lived right next to a ski resort, which I thought was very cool. Skiing was something I had always wanted to do. Skiing was something we were not allowed to do; it is against the Amish religion.

The house where Matt and his mother lived was an older house. After we got to Matt's place, we went into the house, and Matt showed me where the room was that I was going to sleep in for the night.

The room where I slept was very cool. I only had a small blanket to cover up with, and I didn't sleep much at all that night. As I was lying in bed earlier in the morning, I could hear a couple of people talking in the living room. I didn't know who it was, but I assumed it was Matt's mother and one of her friends. I did hear Matt's mother saying how the room that I was sleeping in was a very cool room. As I heard her say how she hoped I stayed warm and slept well.

I had wanted to get up and go sit in the living room where it was warmer. But not knowing Matt's mother, I thought it would be very awkward to sit in the living room with them. Matt's mother's name is Debbie. I had decided to lay in bed until Matt came and woke me up.

After lying there for some time, Matt finally came and knocked on the door, asking me if I was ready to get up. I replied saying I was ready to get up. After I got up, we went into the living room where Debbie and her friend were. Matt introduced me to his mother. Debbie asked me if I slept well and stayed warm. I said yes. I didn't want to tell her any different, as cold as it was. I was just glad that I wasn't sleeping in the back of an old car.

Me and Matt hung out with Debbie and her friend for a while before we left. Debbie had quite a few questions to ask me. She also talked very highly of her son Matt. One of the last things she told me before we left was that if I was to hang out with Matt, I would get to know a lot of great people, and he would also help me with anything I needed. I would say Debbie was pretty well spot on with her words. Me and Matt continued hanging out with each other and still are very good friends with each other to this day.

As the winter was just around the corner, the construction company I was working for during the summer unfortunately didn't have any more work for me. The reason for not getting hired back by the company was that the company did not get much work during the winter time, so hiring me back would not been profitable for the company. I was kind of let down finding out that I was not going to be able to go back to work for the company, as I was now left with having to look for a new job. Being that we were getting into winter and not many places were hiring, plus I also had no identification or social security number, it was not going to be easy getting a good paying job.

I started asking around for jobs or for anybody that was hiring. After some time looking around for a job, I ended up finding a job working on a farm. Working on a farm was not exactly what I had wanted to do, but it was what was available at the time. I had always enjoyed doing farm work when I was still in the community, but after I left, I wanted to do something totally different from farm work. I had actually enjoyed most of the work we had to do when I was growing up, other than having to work in the garden, which was one of my least favorite things to do. However, we had a pretty big garden so me and my siblings and even my parents would work in the garden.

In the Amish community, growing vegetables and selling them was how a lot of the Amish made their main income. Not only do they grow vegetables to sell, they also grow plenty for themself. We would rarely ever buy vegetables from a store. The only vegetable I can remember my father would buy from a store was celery. My father had this thing whenever he was traveling. He would buy celery before he left for the trip. He would bring celery along with him as a snack. Whenever my father would come home with celery, it was a very good sign that he was going to be going away for some time. It would often be going back to Ohio to visit family, or when we had lived in Ohio, he would travel to New York.

My father became a preacher shortly after he and my mother got married. After we moved to New York, my father became a bishop. In the Amish, being a preacher or a bishop, you end up doing more traveling then the rest of the community does. Being a preacher or a bishop is not necessarily easy. If there is any issue in the community, for the most part, it will have to be worked out between the preacher and the bishop. The bishop is pretty well the leader in the community. Most of the time, the bishop will have the final say.

Chapter Four
Amish Churches and Weddings

YOU ALSO DON'T GET TO CHOOSE IF YOU WANT TO be a preacher or a bishop. Every spring and fall, we would have a church session that would only allow for the ones who were baptized, and whenever they would have this church meeting, there was a lot that went on that you didn't find out about if you were not baptized. For me, I was not baptized, and I never found out what it is they do whenever they have this gathering. But I do know whenever someone became a preacher or bishop, it was always when they had this church.

I'm not exactly sure how they went about making someone a preacher or a bishop. You had to be a preacher before you became a bishop. From what I have heard, when they go to make someone a preacher, a group of the younger married men are chosen by the bishop. However, many men were chosen. The bishop would take that many singing books and put a note in one of the books. After he puts the note in the book, he will take all the books, set them on a table, and mix them all up, and even the Bishop himself won't know which book has the note in it. When he gets done mixing them all up, the group of men are asked to come to the table and pick out a book. Whoever picks the book with the note in it becomes a preacher, and it doesn't matter if you don't want to be a preacher. If you pick the book with the note in it, you have to be a preacher, otherwise you would not be accepted in the church. It works pretty well the same way when they make a bishop: However many preachers there were in that church, that is how many books that would be put on the table, and one of the books will have a note in it, and the preacher who gets the book with the note will have to be a bishop. This is done by another bishop.

We also had a Baptist church in the fall; this church was for the ones who were getting baptized. You were usually asked to get baptized when you reach the age of 18 or 19 years old. If I would have stayed Amish, the community would have expected me to get baptized the following summer. Once you are baptized, it means that you have made a commitment to God that you will follow the Amish religion as you are asked to.

This is why I wanted to leave before I got baptized, as I didn't want to make a commitment to God unless I could stand good for my word. I would have not had any issues getting baptized and standing good for my commitment if I would have been able to enjoy my life and fit in with the rest of the community.

Getting baptized was something I had looked forward to do. I had always wanted to grow up being good at following the religion; this was everything I was taught growing up. Not only did I want to do a good job following the religion, I had wanted to be someone who would stand out in the community. In order to do so, you have to be good at what you do. Being a good singer or a good preacher, or even a good worker; if you can grow up to be one of these three things, it will get you to stand out in the community, and they will talk very highly of you. I had always wanted to be one of those people. For me, I had wanted to be a good singer. I practice singing all the time.

I would often be singing whenever I was doing chores in the barn feeding the animals. The animals were the best listeners; they would never talk bad about my singing. And not only would I do a lot of singing, I would do a lot of preaching as well. I had studied the Bible enough that I had memorized quite a lot. I thought if the time came where I ended up being a preacher, I would want to be good at preaching. It didn't matter what it was that I was going to be; I just wanted to be good at doing it. There was this one preacher who had come to our church. His name is Mose. Mose and his family lived around 40 miles away from us. The church was at our house that day. In the Amish, there are no church houses; instead, each family takes turns having the church at their house. Mose and his wife got up early in the morning and drove to our house. They arrived at our house around 8:00 that morning. Our church starts at 9:00, so they made very good time.

He was a very good preacher, and many people in the community talked very well about him. I remember him standing up by the door and preaching for about two hours, and he never had to stop and think what his next word or his next sentences was going to be. In our church, when you stand up to preach, you are not allowed to have the Bible in your hand to read out of; you have to memorize whatever it is you are going to preach that day before you come to church. It is rare that a preacher can stand up by the door and preach without having to stop and think every once in a while what their next word or sentence is going to be.

For Mose to stand up by the door and preach for nearly two hours not having to stop and think what his next word or sentence was going to be, he really stood out in the community. I always thought if I ever became a preacher, I would want to be just like him. For this one Sunday we were in church, the preacher had to skip a few sentences because he could not remember it. I had memorized enough out of the Bible that I knew the part where he had to skip. I felt really proud of myself. It was not usual for a preacher having to skip a sentence simply because he could not remember.

That evening, when we were all gathered around the table to eat dinner, we were just talking about the church. I mentioned that I could have got up and taken over when the preacher had to skip a couple sentences. Everyone at the dinner just kind of laughed. My father told me, "Next time, before the church starts, you can let the preacher know if he is having a hard time to let you know, and you can take over."

Of course, my father was just joking when he said this. If I would have ever said this to a preacher, I would have gotten into a lot of trouble.

As for Mose and his wife, when church got done that day, my father offered them to spend the night at our house since they had got up early in the morning to come to church. It was going to be a very long day for them to travel back home. Not only was it going to be a long day for them, it was also going to be a lot for the horse. You rarely hear of someone traveling over 40 miles in one day with a horse, which was pretty much how far Mose and his wife had traveled.

But Mose and his wife had decided they were going to travel back home that night. This was going to be nearly 80 miles. They traveled in one day, which was the farthest I had heard of anybody traveling in one day with a horse. I remember my father being worried that it would be way too much for the horse. Several weeks went by until we found out how their trip was on their way home. From what we heard, they made it home perfectly fine. Mose and his wife had a couple of their own children who had left the Amish, and it was only several years after they had come to our place for church. When Mose and the rest of his family had decided to leave the Amish community, this was a very big surprise for the Amish community to hear. It was rare to hear a married Amish couple leaving the Amish, and it was pretty well unheard of for a preacher and his family to leave the community. I certainly had never heard of a preacher and his family leaving the community.

There would be times where an Amish family may join another Amish religion, but there are only certain times you would be able to do so. You could only do so when the church had what is called a "split." When an Amish church has a split, you are allowed to join another religion, or you can even leave the community and become an

Englishman, and there is nothing they can do about it or hold anything against you for what choices you make.

When they have a split, the doors are open for anyone that would leave the Amish during this time; as long as you are to join another church, they believe you will make into heaven when your time comes. But when the doors are closed, you are not allowed to leave the community. If you do, they believe when your time comes, you will not make it into heaven. You can also not join another Amish religion during the time the doors are closed. If you were to join another Amish religion, the religion that you wanted to join will not let you join their religion, knowing you are leaving your religion during the time the doors are closed.

During the year of 2001 is when a lot changed under the Swartzentruber Amish. There was a man named Andy Weaver. He decided he was going to start his own church because he did not agree with some of the stuff we were allowed to do. His church was going to be even stricter than what he already was. Surprisingly he got a lot of people to follow him. It was one of the biggest Amish splits ever. Also during that time, there were a lot of teenagers who left the community. You would hear of someone leaving the community every once in a while. Except for this summer, it seemed like every week you heard of someone leaving the community. For the most part, it was the boys who were leaving the community. It was not often you would hear of a girl leaving, and if they did, they would return to the community shortly after they left.

The reason for so many teenagers leaving during that time was because they did not like the idea of having to join a stricter church than they already had. For the ones who were baptized and still living under their parents, rules were given a choice by their parents to either stay the religion that they were in, or they could join the Andy Weaver church. Getting baptized at the age of 18 or 19 years old doesn't mean that you no longer have to obey your parents and live under their rules;

it just means that you have made a commitment to God to follow that religion. You still have to live under your parents' rules until you are the age of 21. The ones who had not been baptized had no choice or say in what church they wanted to be in. Whatever church their parents had chosen to be in, they had to do so as well.

My parents had decided to go to the Weaver church. We had gone long enough to the Weaver church. I had honestly thought that my parents had made a full commitment in joining the Weaver church and so did many of the other Amish in the community. But the last Sunday before the church closed their doors, my parents decided to go back to the church we were before. Whenever the church would have a split, you would have about six months to make up your mind if you wanted to stay or join a different church, as this is roughly how long a split would last. How often would the Amish church have a split? Rarely ever. Some Amish religions pretty well never split. Our church was the Moses church; they had the most split out of all of them.

The first time I remember the church having a split was when I was 10 years old, which was the summer when the Andy Weaver church started. This was the only time our church had a split for the 18 years that I was in the community. The reason they had a split was because one of the bishops had bought an evaporator. The evaporator he bought was to make maple syrup. The evaporator was one of the biggest, if not the biggest evaporator, ever bought under the Amish community, and a lot of the Amish didn't agree with having such a big evaporator. But for others, they didn't see any issues with the evaporator; however, there were enough of the community that didn't agree with having the evaporator that it ended up leading to having a split in the community.

Being that the Amish had such a strict religion it made it very hard for some of them to make a great living. For some, they will struggle for a good part of their life until they get ahead and are able to make a good living. For the ones who would struggle to make ends meet, when they see someone else in the community do very well for themselves, they often get jealous for what they have going for themself. Like buying a big evaporator and being able to produce a lot of maple syrup.

For the ones who would get jealous seeing others doing very well for themselves, they would try to find everything they could to complain to the bishop or to the community. Being it was a bishop who bought the evaporator they didn't agree with, I'm not certain who they complained to.

My uncle, John, was one of those people who did very well for himself. John and his family were considered more on the rich side in the Amish community. A lot of the Amish in that community got very jealous for what John and his family had going for themself. Some of the Amish were saying that they were making too much money and had too many businesses going for themselves for an Amish family.

One of the businesses John had was a harness shop. The community tried to get John to shut down his harness shop. The reason they wanted him to shut down the harness shop was because John was doing a lot of business out of his shop as the harness shop brought in a lot of people from outside the community. The Amish community thought he was doing too much business with people from outside of the community for an Amish family. He was doing a lot of business with non-Amish people. However, if John would have not been making a lot of money the rest of the community would have never said a word. Surprisingly, there are a lot of Amish families who get very jealous seeing others do very well for themself. For some of the families, the reason they struggle for so long is simply because they are on the lazy side or will be convinced that it is hard to make a great living.

Not only are they lazy, they are usually the ones doing all the complaining in the community. For the families who did a lot of complaining, causing all the trouble is what leads to having a split in the community, and also for the families that do a lot complaining, if they were to focus more on their own stuff instead of stirring the pot the Amish community, it would have been a lot more of a peaceful living.

When we would go to church, usually there were several of the elder men who would always be watching us boys and girls to make sure we were behaving ourself. We were not allowed to talk to each other in church. We were not even allowed to smile at each other in church. For the teenage boys, they were always known to get in the trouble the most. For the girls, they were known to behave themself better than the boys did. If you were to smile at someone else in church and one of the elders was to see you, they would tell your parents. If we were caught smiling to someone else and my father would find out, he would get very upset and would want to know why we were smiling and would tell us not to ever do it again or we were going to get a butt spanking. I remember from getting in trouble from church, it wasn't until that evening before I went to bed. I was around the age of 10 or 11 years old. My father was very angry with me. The sad part is that I didn't think I had done anything wrong. One of the older boys had given me a piece of gum.

I waited until after church to chew the piece of gum. I knew I was not allowed to chew gum during church. If someone gave us a piece of gum, we were allowed to chew gum after church; however, my father had decided he did not want me to chew gum during church or after church. My father was so angry with me I thought he was going to give me a butt spanking. He did tell me if I was to do it again, he was going to give me a butt spanking

I was surprised how angry my father was with me. There were other boys my age that would chew gum all the time after church, and they never got in trouble for it. I had often thought about this time, as I couldn't figure out why he was so angry with me. The only reason I could figure out why my father was so angry with me was because it is most likely that something was bothering him a lot, and by taking it out on me, it was going to make him feel better. It often fell to me when my father had anger built up inside him; he would take it out on me or one of my siblings by yelling at us for no reason. I think this was one of those times.

Our church would be around three hours long, sometimes even longer. It would all depend on who was preaching, as some preachers may preach longer than others. Our church had several different preachers. They would take turns to preach; one preacher would preach one Sunday, and the next preacher would preach the next time we went to church. After the church was done, we would eat lunch. Our lunch was more of a simple and easy lunch. We would have what was called "church soup." We would have the same soup every time after church.

Not only did we have church soup, we would also have bread with several different kinds of jam, also beet and canned pickles. This is what we would have every time for lunch after church. The soup was made in a big kettle, either in an iron kettle or stainless kettle. Most of the Amish had an iron kettle, as this is all they used to have, but as time went on, it got harder to find an iron kettle, so the community allowed them to get a stainless kettle.

The soup was made with milk, dried out bread, and white beans. Those who have never had this soup may think that this doesn't sound like a good soup at all. But surprisingly, this is actually a very good tasting soup. I liked the church soup very much. Sometimes my mother would even make it for dinner. I always looked forward to having church soup.

After the soup was done, they would take bigger sized bowls. The bowls would be filled up with soup. After the bowls were filled up, they would put black pepper on top of the soup, and the bowl of soup would be placed on the table. Everyone would gather around the table to eat. There would be several different tables made up for everyone to sit down. We would take two church benches and put them together. After we put them together, we would put a white dishcloth over top of the benches. This would be considered a table. After that, all the food and the silverware would be placed on the table. There would be benches on each side of the table to sit down. As far as getting the table all set up and the food on the table, it was mostly the women who would do that. For the men, they would go outside and visit until someone would call them in for lunch. After we got done eating lunch, we stood around and visited for a while longer until we went home.

I had always enjoyed going to church; however, there was one thing I had enjoyed doing more than going to a church, and that was going to a wedding. In the Amish, when someone gets married, they announce it in church, and two to three weeks after, they announce when they will get married. An Amish wedding is usually quite big, as there are a lot of people invited to an Amish wedding. The wedding is at the girl's house, and she and her family will have to get their place ready for the wedding. They will invite all their cousins and most of their church district. The wedding starts at 8:00 in the morning and will go on all day until 12:00 that evening, which is when the wedding is completely done. As we would all gather together in the morning, it was very similar to going to church. There is a lot of singing and a lot of preaching. The bishop is the one who ends up marrying them. He will stand up by the door and preach for a long time until he calls for the couple to come up and stand in front of him and get married. They usually get married right around 12:00 that day. After they get married, the bishop will continue preaching for a bit longer. When he gets done preaching, he will sit down on the bench, and everyone else will sing for about half an hour or so. When we got done singing, that part of the wedding would be done.

After we got done singing, we would eat lunch. At a wedding, our lunch is a pretty big meal; probably one of the biggest meals the Amish have for any kind of gathering. One of my favorite things we had at the wedding was meatloaf. At every wedding I went to, we always had meatloaf for lunch. As far as I know, meatloaf is something they have at every wedding for lunch.

After everyone got done eating lunch, we would go home to do our evening chores feeding all our animals. Our weddings would be only during the wintertime, and they would also be on Tuesday or Thursday. Getting married on Tuesdays or Thursdays were the only two days of the week that we are allowed to get married, and we were also not allowed to get married during the summer. It would only be from late fall to early spring. Why are we only allowed to get married from late fall to early spring? This is part of the religion as it was probably since the Amish started. In the Amish community, as the younger generation grows up, they continue to follow the religion as they were taught. As time goes on, they rarely ever change any of their religion, and if they do change any of their religion, it is actually to have a stricter religion.

However, as for the wedding, after we went home and did all our evening chores, then we would go back to the wedding place. This is when the evening wedding started. Not only did we have to do the evening chores since it was during the winter time, we also had to fill up the wood stove. Our house was heated with wood, and we wanted it to be nice and warm when we got back from the wedding later that evening.

For the elders, they would usually stay at the wedding place. For us children, we would usually be the ones having to go home and do the chores. Most of the older couples that were pretty well retired would only have a couple horses and maybe a few cows, so it was easier for them to hire the neighbor to do their chores. For everyone who stayed at the wedding place waiting for everyone to come back from doing their chores, they would all gather around the table and sing. There was certainly a lot of singing in the wedding. For the ones who had stayed at the wedding and sat at the table to sing, there were always several bowls of candy bars they passed around the table. The candy bars were as a treat. If you were one of the people who went home to do chores, you did not get a candy bar. I had always wanted to be able to stay and get a candy bar. It was very rare that we got candy bars, and it was a very big treat when we did.

It wasn't until I was around the age of 15 that I was able to stay all afternoon and didn't have to go home to do evening chores. This was only because one of our cousins was getting married; they lived about 40 miles from us. It was only me, my brother Dan, and my parents who had gone to the wedding. For the rest of my siblings, they stayed at home to take care of the chores. Since the wedding was so far from our place, we had traveled to our cousin's place the day before and spent the night at their house.

We also spent the night at their house after the wedding and traveled back home the next day. For our cousins, they had quite a lot of animals to feed. I decided to go out in the barn and help them feed their animals. As we were out in the barn doing the chores, one of the men who was in the house came out to the barn with a bowl of candy bars to pass around to everyone who was doing chores in the barn. When I saw the man come walking down the barn toward us with a bowl of candy bars, I was very excited when he passed the bowl to me. I started going through the bowl to find a candy that I would like. The worst part was, there was not one candy bar in the bowl that I liked. There were only Hershey candy bars in the bowl. I ended up picking out one of the candy bars. I only took a few bites of the candy bar and threw the rest of the candy bar away.

There was something about Hershey candy bars that would make me very sick if I was to eat the whole candy bar. Even a couple bites gave me a belly ache. As excited as I was to get a candy bar, I was very disappointed not being able to get a candy bar that I liked. After all the chores got done and everyone who had gone home to do chores all came back to the place where the wedding was, we all gathered around the table to have dinner.

In an Amish wedding, there are enough people who show up that the family will pretty well take all the furniture out of their house and set their house all up with tables. They will even set up tables in the basement, and for some, they close their porch and have tables set up on their porch.

For the most part, all the tables will be full. After dinner gets done, all the married men and women they will stay seated around the table and sing. Dinner would usually be completely done by 8:00. The men and women who stay seated around the table will sing until 11:00 or maybe even a little later than that. When they get done singing, the tables in the living room and kitchen will be set up for what is called the Midnight Table. The Midnight Table is for all the ones that were rumspringa.

All the boys and girls who are old enough to be rumspringa all gather together in the basement and play a game until it is time to go sit at the midnight table. The game that we played, I'm not exactly sure what the name of the game is called. I'm not even sure that game has a name. I went to a couple weddings where I was old enough to go in the basement and play the game until it was time to go sit at the Midnight Table. I never heard a name for the game. The way the game is played is a little bit on the weird side. There are benches set up in the basement for us to sit down. The guys sit on one side and the women sit on the other side. The way we are seated, we are facing each other.

In between us is where the game is played. There is be a guy and a girl who stand together, and they put their arms on each other's shoulder, and then one of the guys goes up to one of the girls and snaps his fingers, she has to follow him over to where the guy and the girl are standing with their arms on each other's shoulder. The girl chases him around the guy and girl until she tags him. If I was the guy who snapped a girl, after she tagged me, I then would have to take the guy's place who's standing with his arm around the first girl, and the girl who tagged me would snap one of the boys, and then the guy tagged her, then she would take the girl's place, and so the game continued like that until it was time to go sit at the Midnight Table.

The first time I went to a wedding when I was old enough to be rumspringa, I had no idea what it was they did in the basement. Nobody told you. You have to find out for yourself. I still remember the first time a girl came up and snapped me. This girl was close to my age, and she was very talkative. I was very shy and didn't talk much at all. She was not shy at all. I remember her having a few different conversations with me, and I would try to talk along the best I could. My sister Mary had also been at the wedding, and she and the girl who had snapped me were sitting right next to each other. I could hear them talk to each other quite a bit as I even heard them talking about me. However, I was not able to hear what they were saying. I just remember hearing my sister telling her my name. It seemed to me like the girl may like me. As the night went on, it came to a point where it was my turn to snap one of the girls, so I decided to snap her.

When the time came where it was time to go sit at the Midnight Table, you had to choose a girl to take to the Midnight Table and sit next to you. If you choose a girl and she decides she doesn't want to go to the midnight table and sit next to you, she could say no. She could also say who she wanted to go to the Midnight Table with. I had decided to choose the girl who had snapped me for the first time since it seemed to me that she may like me. I thought it would be a great idea to pick her to take to the Midnight Table. She agreed to go with me to the Midnight Table. After all the guys and girls picked out who they were going to the midnight table with, we would all gather around the table and sing a few songs. If there were more women than guys and they didn't get chosen by someone to go to the Midnight Table with, they would have to be the table waiter. It was the same when there were more guys than women, and they didn't get chosen; the guys would have to be the waiters. Being a waiter at the midnight table is very simple. Filling up the glasses with water was probably the hardest part. By the time we had all gathered around the table to sing, it was pretty well 12:00. This is why it is called the Midnight Table.

We did have a few more conversations at the table with each other, and I did find myself liking the girl quite a bit. However, after that night, I never did see her again. She and her family lived far enough away that we were not in the same church. This was shortly after I turned 17. I could have written her a letter. I would have to have my parents promise to do so. The only way that I would have got to see her or if I wanted to have a date with her, I would have had to travel to her area by bus. Since I had only been 17 years old, my father wouldn't have let me go visit her very often. He would have allowed me to go visit her maybe once a year.

This was one of those times where I also wonder if my father didn't have such strict rules if I still would be living the Amish life.

However, the reason it didn't work was probably because it was not meant to be. One of the reasons my father would not have let me travel to her community very often was because traveling by bus costs money, so my father would have to pay for my bus ride. For my father, he would have much rather had me find someone in our community to date. But as time goes on and everything is working against you to enjoy your life, you start looking for other options, which is just what happened for me.

That evening, after the wedding got done, I had decided to spend the night at my cousin Elmer's place. I rode with him to their place; Elmer had a very wild horse. That night, after we got the horse all hitched up to the buggy, we started going down the road. Elmer's horse had so much energy, he had all he could do to keep his horse under control. We came to the end of a road, where we had to turn onto another road, we were going way too fast to make the turn. Elmer was not able to slow the horse down enough to make the turn. We ended up flipping the buggy over. Lucky enough, neither one of us got hurt, and when the buggy flipped over, the horse came to a complete stop. Me and Elmer were able to get the buggy back on its wheels. The buggies are light enough that two people can lift it back on its wheels if it flips over.

Several years after I had left the community, Elmer also left the community. We never really got to hang out with each other outside the community. We were living pretty far apart from each other, and at the time, Elmer was moving around quite a bit, and I was also doing my fair share of moving around. This is why we did not get to hang out with each other on the outside of the community.

CHAPTER FIVE
GARDENING AND DOING FIELD WORK

D URING THE SUMMER TIME, it was certainly a much busier time for the community with growing all the vegetables and also growing plenty of food for all the animals as well. Working in the fields doing field work was something I had enjoyed a lot. All the field work had to be done with horses. We are not allowed to use any kind of tractors or any kind of motorized equipment to do our field work. It had to be done with horses. We had to make sure we had plenty of grain to store in the barn to feed our animals, enough to last them through the winter. For the most part, we were able to do so. There were a few times when we had to buy hay to last the animals through the winter. When that was the case, we would buy hay from the English. The reason we couldn't buy hay from another Amish family is because most of the Amish only produce enough for their own animals.

For ourselves, we canned plenty of vegetables and meat to last us through the winter. We had a pretty good-sized garden. We had 500 strawberry plants. During the strawberry season, we got up a little earlier in the morning, so we could go out and pick the strawberries before it got really hot out. Picking strawberries was probably one of my least favorite things to do. Picking strawberries was something that took a long time to do, as it was not a very fast process. For me, after several hours of picking strawberries, I would get very bored and was ready to do something else. But we had to stay in the garden until the strawberries were all picked.

As far as doing garden work, picking sweet corn was one of my favorite things to do. Picking sweet corn was something that went pretty quick. Whenever we got done working in the garden in the morning, us boys would either go work in the field for the rest of the day or go work in the sawmill. We were lucky enough to have a sawmill and were able to cut logs and sell the lumber, so we didn't have to just depend on growing vegetables for our living. During the summer time, working in the garden and the sawmill we stay pretty busy. With all the vegetables that we sold plus all the business we did in the sawmill, we did fairly well as far as making a decent income.

For those who were mostly depending on their livelihood of growing vegetables and selling them, some years it may not necessarily work in their favor. If the weather didn't cooperate just right, it could be a bad year for growing vegetables. So, for the families that were mostly depending on their income from the vegetables, if it was a bad year for growing vegetables, those families may be left struggling to make ends meet during the winter. In the Amish community, if you struggle to make ends meet, you don't get any help from the church. The only help you may get is from your own families. If someone in your family is doing quite well financially, you may be able to borrow money from them. It is rare for someone outside the family to lend money to you. However, there are times where it does happen. But for the most part, you are left with having to figure out your financial situation on your own. There was this one family in our church where their financial situation got so bad, they ended up not having any money at all. They were completely broken.

In the Amish community, when there is a family that ends up being completely broke. the two older men in the community who are not a preacher or bishop will be the ones that will help the family out by going to their place and basically making the decisions for them and controlling their money. This is the one thing that the bishop won't get involved with much. They go to the family place almost every day until the family starts doing better financially. Whenever an Amish family gets to the point where they are broke, it is most likely they have managed to borrow money from their own family to the point where the family would tell them they will no longer lend them money, and they have to find out how to make ends meet on their own. How often does it happen that an Amish family is completely broke? Not very often. I had only known several different families it had happened to.

A lot of the Amish families, when they are struggling to make ends meet, will for the most part lean on their parents for money. But if the parents don't have much money to begin with and no one else in the family has enough money to lend to you, the family starts looking to borrow money from someone outside their family.

Several years after I left, a couple different Amish families asked me to borrow money from me. The families were having hard times making ends meet. For me, knowing how hard it is to make ends meet in the Amish, I felt bad for the family and decided to lend them money. It wasn't like I had a lot of money, but I knew that for the families to go as far as asking me to lend money, they were running out of options to lend money from their family or anyone else in the community. By the time, I got done lending the money to the families, I barely had any money left over for myself. But I figured they probably needed the money more than I did.

During the time that I did lend money to those families, I wasn't making much money; just enough to get by. The money I loaned to them was money I had saved up. It is rare that I would ever lend money to someone. But seeing a family or anyone struggling to make ends meet, I do feel bad for those families, and I like to see everyone doing good. So by lending them the money they needed at the time, I thought I was doing a great thing, and I felt very confident that I would get the money back at some point.

However, as for getting the money back, it didn't go like I thought it would. The one family repaid me within a year, but for the other family, it was over four years until I got all my money back. The only reason I got my money back was because after three years I decided to go to the family home asking to have my money returned. After going back to the family house off and on for about a year and asking to have my money returned, they finally repaid me. Not only did I think I was doing a good thing by helping these families out, I also thought it would help build somewhat a relationship with the Amish community. Even though I have left the community, I still like to be somewhat involved with the community and knowing what is going on in the community. I had known that the elders in the community would not approve for the families to borrow money from me, but it is not against their religion to borrow money from someone outside the community. As far as me thinking it would help build a relationship with the community, I was wrong. After the family repaid me, it was just like before; nobody in the community wanted to have any part of me coming around.

This was also not the first time I had loaned money to an Amish family and had a hard time having my money returned. After realizing that it was not helping me build a relationship with the community, I decided I was never going to lend money to anyone in the Amish community ever again, as it did bother me a lot that part of me felt like all they did was take advantage of me. After I had left the community, one of my biggest fears was not having any money to take care of myself. It was not like I could go back to my parents asking for money if it ever came to the point where I was having a hard time making ends meet. Certainly no one in my family was going to help me out.

There were certain states where the Amish did quite well for themself, certainly a lot better than other states did. Pennsylvania, Ohio, and Indiana are known for having a lot of Amish communities. In certain areas, it is very heavily populated with Amish. When we had lived in Ohio, the area we had lived in was pretty well all Amish. And as far as financial-wise, the Amish in Ohio seem to do very well for themself. Definitely better than they did in New York. When we lived in Ohio, we would grow a lot of vegetables. There were several different auctions that were not too far from our place. These auctions were called "product auctions." We would take our vegetables to the auction and sell them. There were a lot of the Amish who did this, and for the most part, we would get paid very well for our vegetables.

After we had moved to New York, there were no product auctions. The only way for us to sell vegetables was to sell them on the side of the road. We built a vegetable stand at the end of our driveway. We would pick our vegetables and put them in the stand to sell. It involved doing a lot of work, getting the garden ready, and planting the vegetables then attending to them till they were ready. After we picked the vegetables and put them in the stand to sell, all we could do was hope there would be enough people stopping by our stand to buy our vegetables, so we could somewhat make a halfway decent living.

There was one thing that we sold a lot more than we did when we lived in Ohio. That was baked goods. The first summer we moved to New York, my mother had decided to start baking bread and pies and put it out beside the road to sell. We ended up doing very well. My mother and my sister Mary would bake every Thursday to sell on Friday and Saturday. We were not allowed to do any business on Sunday. We could give someone a loaf of bread or a pie or anything else we wanted to, but we were not allowed to sell anything. My mother and Mary would spend pretty well all-day Thursday baking as I can remember. We would sell around 70 loaves of bread in two day and over 20 pies, sometimes even more. We were very surprised to see how many people stopped by our house to buy baked goods. One of the reasons we were so surprised to sell so many baked goods was because we did not live on a main road; we lived on a side road where not many people would travel by.

Not only did we live off a side road, we also lived pretty far out in the country. The closest town was about five miles away. The town was small enough where some people may not even consider it a town. However, the word spread very fast throughout the outside of the Amish community that we were selling baked goods, which we were very thankful for. The first summer we moved to New York, we built a barn and by having the extra income coming in by selling baked goods was a big help.

When we moved to New York, we moved to an area where there were only two other Amish families living there. They had moved there about a month before we did. As time went on, there were more Amish families who moved in the area. We were one of the first families to bake and sell baked goods on the side of the road in our area. But it wasn't long until the other Amish families in the community saw the amount of business we were doing by selling baked goods, so they started doing the same. As more families moved into the community, pretty much all of the Amish in our area would bake and sell baked goods on the side of the road, and this, of course, was giving us less business. But as far as financial-wise, my mother and father always seemed to figure out a way to make ends meet and not have to struggle for money like some of the Amish families did. My parents always seemed to do very well for themself by doing business from our home. There are quite a few of the Amish who are able to do so, but for some, they are not so lucky.

One of the things I had always liked about all the baking my mother did was, for the most part, what we didn't sell all of the baked goods that was left over, we got to eat. My mother had also started making cookies to sell as well, but for me, I was never a big fan of cookies. Eating pies was something I liked very much. Strawberry rhubarb pie was my favorite and still is to this day. We didn't get to have many strawberry rhubarb pies for ourself as they were very good sellers. But we did get to have plenty of other pies.

As far as having food to eat, for the most part the Amish eat very well. There was always plenty of food on our table, and there were always left over. When I had left and had to go back until I was 18, I remember my father asking me if I left because I wasn't getting enough food, but that certainly was not why I had left. My mother was a very good cook, and there are many days that I think of my mother's cooking and wish things were a lot easier for me to have somewhat of a relationship with my family, so I could go home and have a meal with my family ever once in a while.

But I am very lucky and grateful to have friends who treat me like family and invite me to go to their place and have a meal with them every once in a while. I pretty much did not do any cooking when I was living at home, nor did I know how until sometime after I left. I had never realized how much work it was to cook food for just one meal.

The first time I can remember trying to cook a meal was when I was the age of 15. I was home by myself, and I think it was the first time I was home by myself. When lunchtime came around, I went into the house to make something for lunch. As I was walking into the house, I started thinking about what I was going to make for lunch. I started going through the food pantry, trying to find something that I could make for lunch. I knew it had to be something very simple, otherwise I was not going to be able to make it. I ended up finding a pack of hotdogs, which it was very rare that we would have hotdogs, but it just so happened that we had hotdogs at the time. As I thought to myself, *I can make hotdogs*. But I came to find out that I could not even make hotdogs. It was the first time I had tried to cook or make anything, and nobody had ever shown me how to make hotdogs or any other kind of food. I opened up the pack of hotdogs and put them in a dish and put it on top of the stove. After I had put them on top of the stove, I went back in the pantry looking for what else I could have for lunch, thinking that it would take a while for the hotdogs to get done. After some time going through the pantry, I didn't really find anything else to have with the hotdogs. I went back into the kitchen to check on the hotdog. The hotdog had pretty well been burned. Way too burnt to eat. By this time, I was very disappointed in myself. I knew if I couldn't make hotdogs, I certainly was not going to be able to make anything else.

I took the hotdogs and threw them out. I didn't want anyone in my family to find out. I was worried that I might get picked on for not knowing how to make hotdogs. It wasn't until a few years after I had left the community that I found out that when you make hotdogs all you have to do is put water in a dish and then put it on top of the stove, and went the hotdogs float to the top, that is when they are ready.

I'm not certain what I ate after I threw away the hotdogs. I know whatever I had was certainly not much. In the Amish community, the men work out in the field, and as for the women, they pretty much work in the house and do all the cooking, cleaning, and laundry as well. The only one of my brothers who knew how to do some cooking was my brother Ura. but for the rest of my brothers, they were pretty much as clueless when it came to cooking as I was. This was also the first time I had realize how much work there is in making food, as I was just trying to make food for myself, and I thought to myself, *I can't imagine how much work it would be to cook for 12 people!* With my parents and all my brothers and sisters, this is how many there were in our family. It wasn't unusual for someone to complain if there was food on the table that they didn't like. My father was someone who did his fair share of complaining if there was food on the table that he didn't like. For the most part, the food that he didn't like, my mother wouldn't make if he was home because my father would get upset. However, if there was food that me and my siblings didn't like, if my father liked it and if it was on the table, he would make us eat it.

Tomato was something that only a few of my siblings liked. For the rest of us, we did not like tomatoes. But if we had tomatoes on the table, our father would make us eat them with our meal. After I had realized how much work there was to making a meal, I tried to do my best to never complain about the food as I knew it is not easy to cook for 12 people and hoped they all liked it. Whenever someone would complain about the food, I would always feel bad for my mother and sister, as I knew it was a lot of work to make a meal.

Not only did I enjoy gathering around the table to have a meal with my family, I had always enjoyed going to visit another family. We would get to stay at their place for a meal. It had excited me to see what we would have to eat. There was usually something different on the table than we had at home, and sometimes there would be food on the table that I had never tried, which would always excite me. One of the things that I always wanted to try, which our neighbor made it when we lived in Ohio, was homemade pizza. My father and a couple of my brothers had it, and they would always talk about how good the pizza was. They would describe it as "the best pizza they ever had." It was one of the only things that I really wanted to try. However, I never did get to try the neighbor's homemade pizza.

In the Amish, when one family goes to visit another family, they will do it on Sunday that they don't have to go to church, and for the most part, we would always stay for a meal. It would usually be for lunch. But sometimes it would be at suppertime. This is not the only time we get to eat at another family house. When the Amish go to build a house or a barn or any other kind of building they may build for themselves, the community will gather together to help the family build whatever it is they are building, unless the family would decide to do it on their own, which is only when they are building smaller buildings. As far as a house or barn, the community and even a lot of the relatives would gather together to help them. This was also something I had enjoyed doing very much. You would get to see many people and even meet new people.

Not only would you get to meet new people, when lunch time came around, everyone would gather together and have lunch. Whenever the community would gather together to build a building it was called a "frolic." Going to frolic was something pretty much all the Amish enjoyed doing. Not only did I like to go to the frolic and get to meet new people. I liked the idea of being able to eat food off someone else's table. I would always make sure I would get my fair share of food, which was the case for pretty much all Amish, as they are very big eaters. After I had left the community, I had found myself where I would not eat nearly as much food as I did when I was still in the community.

The Amish are very good cooks. Sitting at a table with a lot of great food on the table, it is very easy to stuff yourself full unless the family is not very clean. However, most of the Amish are very clean. It was rare that it would bother me to sit at another Amish family's table to eat food. I had always looked forward to eating at another family table other than this one family. After we had moved to New York, I still remember the first time I had sat at their table to eat a meal. They had a frolic that me and one of my brothers went to. As I was eating away, I came to find out that they are not very clean at all. I ended up finding a hair in the food, which I didn't think much of, other than it kind of grossed me out. But I didn't say a word, I just kept eating away. It was not long after I found a fly in my food. By this time, I was no longer hungry for food. A few of the other guys also found a fly in their food, and by the time I got done eating, I felt like I could go outside and throw up. I remember thinking to myself that, *I hope I never have to eat at this family's house ever again.* They became known in the community for not being a very clean-living family. Even some of their own family would talk about how they were not very clean. Whenever they had a church, of course, we all had to go. After the church got done, we had to stay for lunch. They were the last family I wanted to stay for lunch. However, I had no choice. Whenever the church was at their place, I would eat as little as possible. Usually I would eat mostly just bread and jam.

The Amish would always buy bread from a grocery store for the church. It was just too much work making enough bread for everyone plus all the other food they had to make. So by buying bread, it made it easy for them to prepare for church. They would still have some homemade bread on the table, as some did prefer the homemade bread over the store-bought bread. When the church was at this family's house, I was definitely eating store-bought bread and store-bought only. The main meal in the church is the bean soup, which I happen to like very much unless it was at this family's house, then I would barely eat any soup. I was not the only one either. The soup is made on the day of church and usually someone in the family will help you make the soup.

I remember one of the first times we went to the family's house for church. As I was sitting at the table barely eating any soup and seeing others doing the same, I thought to myself, *I wonder what they use to clean out the kettle before they make the soup in it, or if they even clean it out...* The family brother Henry had helped them make the soup that Sunday. Henry and his family was very clean, but as for his sister's family, they were just the opposite. Henry and his wife were pretty good friends with my parents, and they would stop by to visit quite often. Henry and his family stopped by to visit us several weeks after his sister's family had the church. While they were at our place visiting, something got brought up about his sister's family not being a very clean-living family. Henry said when he was helping them make soup for the church that the kettle was not very clean at all. Henry said that they used a towel to clean out the kettle. The towel they used was not a clean towel; it was a towel their children used the night before after they got done taking a bath. Just thinking about it made me want to throw up. The Amish are not allowed to have showers. We are only allowed to take baths. We would heat our water up in the iron kettle and then put it in the bathtub. There are around four or five kids that will use the same water before they change it. And the same goes when it comes to using a towel. So the towel they used to clean their kettle, four or five of their children used the night before when they got done taking a bath.

We also only take a bath once a week. It would be on Saturday evening, so we would be clean to go to church or if we were just hanging out at home. During the summertime, when it was really hot, we would take a bath twice a week. But during the cold part of the winter, we would only take a bath once every two weeks.

Winter is something the Amish enjoy a lot. They like to see when it snows and when it snows a lot. During the wintertime was a very slow time, and there was not much to do. One of the reasons we liked the winter so much was because we like to ride a sled down the hill or toboggan. This is what me and my siblings would do during the wintertime when we were not busy working. As far as the work we had to do during the wintertime, it was pretty much just doing our chores. That was the main thing we had to do during the wintertime. The other thing we did for work during the wintertime was cutting firewood for the next winter.

We had a bigger sized bobsled. The bobsled that we had was to hook the horses to it. We would go out in the woods, cut firewood, and load it onto the bobsled, then bring it out in the meadow, so when it did warm up, it had a great place to dry. We were not allowed to use chainsaws. Our firewood would have to be cut by hand. Working in the woods during the wintertime was something I had enjoyed doing, as it was very peaceful work. We did not get to do this when we lived in Ohio. Most of our wood that we use to heat our house was bought, and we would also buy some coal. We had mostly all farmland when we lived in Ohio. We certainly did not have enough wooded land to cut wood from our land to heat our house during the winter time.

In the early 2000s, my parents started looking for land in New York. By 2004, they had bought land in New York, and there was plenty of wooded land. My parents bought around 200 acres. There were over 100 acres of wooded land, so we had plenty of wooded land to cut firewood from to supply all of our heat that we needed.

CHAPTER SIX
MOVING FROM OHIO TO NEW YORK

M OVING FROM OHIO TO NEW YORK was something I didn't want to do. This one winter, my father made quite a lot of trips to New York. One of his trips, when he came home and said that he bought land in New York, and we were going to be moving by spring. My father made one more trip to New York before we moved. This time, he had Dan go with him. There was only a house on the property that my father bought. He wanted to build a pole barn before we moved, so we had a place to put some of our stuff under a roof. I was in the seventh grade in school and had quite a few friends. I was worried if we moved, I would never get to see my friends again, or at least not for a long time. As springtime started coming around, we were very busy packing all of our stuff. Some of our neighbors and some of our cousins would come and help us pack our stuff. As for the women, they were very busy working in the house getting everything packed and ready to go.

All of our food was canned in the glass jars; all the glass jars were wrapped in the newspaper. After we had it all wrapped, we put it in 55 gallons of barrels. We packed as many canning jars in a barrel as we could. After it was full, whatever space was left in the barrel would get filled up with oats, so the canning jars could not move around. The oats were something we grew in our fields. We grew the oats to feed our horses, so by putting the oats in the barrels to fill up the extra space, after we unpacked the barrels, the oats could be used to feed the horses. The oats ended up working really well from what I can remember when we went to unpack the canning jars. They had all been good; none of them had broken.

We had quite a few canning jars. I'm not sure how many, but if I had to guess it would be somewhere around 400. As the women stayed busy packing stuff in the house, the men stay busy getting all the outdoor equipment ready. Not only were we busy getting ready to move, but my parents decided to have an auction and sell all the stuff that we didn't want to move to New York with us.

My parents had decided to have an auction because we had way more stuff than we wanted to pack up and move to New York with us, so as we were going through all of our stuff packing up, we also had to separate the stuff we didn't want to take to New York with us. There was some household stuff that we sold, but we sold a lot of our farm equipment and also most of our cattle. We only brought several of our cattle to New York with us. I still remember very easily the day we had our auction. It was a very damp and rainy day. There were many people who showed up to the auction; even some of our cousins from New York had come to the auction. In the Amish, going to an auction is something they enjoy doing.

One of the things I remember being sold was one of our cows. Her name was Tiny, and I had always liked Tiny a little more than the rest of our cows. The reason was because it seemed like almost every time she would have a calf, it would be twins. I always looked forward to seeing her having calves. She was the only cow that I can remember that would have twins. But my parents had decided we had way too many animals to move to New York with us. We did keep three cows that we brought to New York with us, but sadly, Tiny was one of the cows who got sold in the auction.

I enjoyed the day of the auction a lot. Some of my friends from school were there, and I got to hang out with them. I kept thinking to myself once we moved to New York, I probably would not get to see them for a long time.

On the day of the auction, we did not gather around the table to eat when lunchtime came. This is probably one of the only things the Amish have that they do not gather around the table to eat during lunchtime. Instead, we had a cater that came in. They set up in our basement. You can easily go into our basement from outside of our house, so it was a great place for people to go to eat food and be out of the weather.

We would always eat lunch at 11:30. But on the day of the auction, I had no idea what I was supposed to do for food. The only way I was getting food from the catering was if I had money, which was something I didn't have. I kept thinking of all the ways that I could get money to buy food. However, I never did find a way to come up with money. As time went on, I kept thinking about food only because I was hungry. It got to be midafternoon, and I decided to go ask my father if he would give me money, so I could go get some food. My father was very busy at the time. He was busy pretty well all day. He was right next to the auctioneer to make sure all of our stuff would get sold at a decent price. If something was going to be sold and was way underpriced, my father was going to keep it for himself. Since my father was standing next to the auctioneer and there was a big crowd of people standing around the auctioneer, I ended up having to find my way through the crowd to get to my father.

When I got to my father, I took my hand and tapped him on the back. He turned around to see who it was. When he saw who it was, he asked me what it was that I wanted. I told my father I was hungry and was wondering if I could have some money to buy some food. My father didn't give me any money; instead, he said to just wait a little longer. He was going to get some food for himself, and when he was going to do that, he was going to buy food for me and some of my other siblings.

It ended up being pretty late in the afternoon until we ended up getting food. Not only was I hungry, I was also excited to eat food that was not considered a home cooked meal. It was rarely ever that we had food that was not made at home. In the Amish, having a non-home cooked meal was like a very big treat. The caterer also had ice cream brought with him, which was also something we would rarely ever have, unless it was during the wintertime, when we would sometimes make our own ice cream. I was looking forward to getting ice cream all day.

My father buying food for all of us plus buying ice cream for all of us was not going to happen. As far as what the caterer had for food, it was mostly hotdogs and hamburgers, and for the drinks, there was soda or water. I don't remember what my father bought for me and my siblings to eat, but I remember it was not much. It would either have been a hamburger or a hotdog and no ice cream. We did eat dinner later that evening, but I still wished I could have had some ice cream. After the auction was done, everyone had pretty well gone home, except some of our cousins who had come from New York. They ended up spending the night.

After the auction was all over, it was only a couple weeks away until we were moving to New York. Everything started feeling very different around home. Our barn and tool shop felt very empty; it just wasn't feeling like the same place anymore, which makes me feel a little on the sad side. For the next couple of weeks, there was not much to do other than doing our chores and making sure all of our stuff was ready to go when the day came that we were moving to New York.

It seemed like everything was going faster than I had wanted it to go. I had not wanted to move to New York at all. We were moving 500 miles away from where we were currently living. The area where we were moving to, there were only a couple other Amish families living there at the time. For me and my siblings, we had never met them before. We were moving 500 miles away to an area where we did not know anybody and didn't have any friends.

When the morning came that we were moving, we had to get up extra early that morning as a lot of the neighbors were gathering together that day to help us move. My father had hired a guy from New York who had a trucking company. They came to pick up all of our stuff. The trucking company showed up with two different tractor trailers; one of the trucks was a box truck, which was the truck we put all of our household stuff in, and the other truck was for all the farm equipment. Both trucks showed up very early in the morning. It was just starting to break daylight when they showed up.

Our driveway was very narrow and long; we probably lived around half a mile from the road. Our neighbor had a sawmill at the end of our driveway. My father asked the neighbor if it would be okay if the trucks parked at the sawmill, since there was a pretty good size parking lot. The neighbor said it would be fine to park the trucks at the sawmill for the day since our driveway was narrow, and the trucks were not going to be able to fit down our driveway.

It worked out great for us that we were able to park at the sawmill. The only downside was that we had to load all of our stuff in a wagon and bring it to the sawmill and then load it in the trucks. We had two different wagons. We had a team of horses hooked to each wagon and even some of the neighbors brought a team of horses and their wagons to help bring stuff out to the trucks, which was a very big help for us. I enjoyed the day very much. I was having fun helping load stuff onto the wagon and then bringing it out to the sawmill to load in the trucks. The reason I was having fun was because most of the friends that I was going to school with were also there. We probably did as much playing around with each other as we did working. It took pretty well all day to bring all of our stuff out to the trucks.

At the end of the day, as all my friends were getting ready to go home, I shook all of their hands, and as I was shaking all of their hands, I told them this handshake would have to last for a long time, as I didn't know when the next time would be that I would get to see them. In the Amish, we do not give hugs when we say goodbye to someone; it is just a handshake, and that is all. We never said "I love you," as that is just not a thing in the Amish community.

As I was giving my friends a handshake, I thought I would certainly get to see them again. I did think it would be several years before it would happen. However, after that handshake, that was the last time I got to see them. I often think of that handshake and how sad it is that I never got to hang out with them again.

After I said goodbye to my friends, they left to go home. I went back to the house where the rest of my siblings were. We had to pack all of our clothes in a suitcase. We were leaving later that evening to go catch the bus. In the Amish, if we would travel a long distance, we were allowed to travel by bus or train, but if we were just going to town we had to travel by horse and buggy.

Before we left, one of our cousins came walking into the house to say goodbye to all of us. His name is Menno. Me and some of my brothers were in the living room standing next to the wood stove. Menno came walking into the living room, and he visited with us for a while before saying goodbye. One of the last things he told us before he left was that the next year will be a very hard time for us, and we were going to miss our friends so much that there will be times where we will have tears in our eyes.

After Menno left and when home, I thought to myself there was no way I would ever miss someone so much that I would cry. At the moment, I didn't have much time to think much of anything as we had to be ready to leave at a certain time that evening. I don't remember who ended up bringing us to the bus station. I just remember it being almost dark by the time we got to the bus station. The one thing I kept thinking about was how empty our house was before we left. I had never seen a house looking so empty. I think the only thing left in the house was the stove in the living room.

There was another Amish family who had already bought our place before we left, which had made it nice for my parents. They didn't have to worry about finding someone to buy our place after we left. The farm was in our family for quite a few years. My grandparents had bought the farm after they got married. This was the same farm my father and all his brothers and sisters grew up with. But the time came where my grandparents had decided to buy a farm in New York and move to New York, and so did all my father's siblings. My parents had decided that they would stay in Ohio and take over the family's farm. It was around 20 years after my grandparents moved to New York that my parents started having interest in buying a farm in New York and moving to New York.

After we got to the bus station, we waited for a little while until the bus showed up. For me, I was looking forward to going for a bus ride. We would rarely ever get to go for a ride in a motorized vehicle. The only other time I got to ride in a car one was when I had to go to the hospital, so I thought the bus ride would be fun.

At first the bus ride went very well. My brother Ura and I were sitting next to each other. I was sitting next to the window. I was very excited that I got to sit next to the window. As I thought, *I get to look out the window and get to see a lot of different things along the way…* I realized I was not able to see much because it was very dark, unless we were going through a city, which was something I had never got to do before.

As we were making our way toward New York, occasionally we would have to stop at a bus station and get onto another bus. One of the bus stations we stopped at, I remember from sitting in a chair and seeing a TV hanging on the wall, and it was turned on. I don't remember what it was playing, but this was the first time I watched tv. After several hours of being on the bus, my brother Ura started getting sick to the point where he had to throw up. He was sick for quite some time, and every once in a while, he would throw up. At first, it didn't seem to bother me at all. After about four to five hours of Ura being sick and throwing up every once in a while, he started feeling better. As things started getting better for my brother Ura, things started to get worse for me. I started getting sick and throwing up. I didn't get sick for just four to five hours though. I ended up getting really sick and throwing up for the rest of the way to New York, and I was even sick for three days after we arrived. We arrived at our new place around 2:00 the next day. I was very glad when we arrived. All I wanted was to find a bed to lay down and sleep, which is just what I did after we arrived at our new place.

I walked into the house not to look around at our new home. I was looking around to find a bed to lay down. All I had on my mind was to find a bed. I ended up finding the stairs to go upstairs. I thought that would be my best bet, to go upstairs where it would be quieter, and also where no one was really going to see me or try to talk to me. As I got to the top of the stairs, there was a door on the right-hand side that I walked into. I didn't know if there were going to be any beds set up or not. But luckily enough, there was a bed all set up in the room. I didn't even bother looking around the rest of the upstairs to see how it looked. I just went and laid in bed. I lay in bed until the next morning. I was so sick, I was not able to get up to go eat dinner that night. Even if I would have been able to eat dinner, I probably would have ended up throwing up. As for the next three days, I barely ate any food. I would get up and go sit at the table when it was time to eat. It wasn't until after the third day until I started feeling much better and eating more.

As I was getting to feel better, I started to go outside and help with work. One of the first things I remember doing was having to go to the neighbor to get water. The place we had bought was from an English family, and it was all set up with electricity. Since the Amish are not allowed to use electricity, we had no way of getting water from the well. There were water pipes that went from the well to the basement. The only way for us to get water from this well was with a water pump set up to a small gas power engine, which was something we were allowed to have. Most of the Amish family have a hand water pump set up in the house by the sink, and that was how we would get our water by hand pumping. In this house, we were not able to do so. After several days, we were able to get the water pump and a small engine set up, so we did not have to go to the neighbors.

The neighbor where we were getting the water from is an English family. As time went on, we got to know them very well. There were times where we would invite them to have dinner with us, and then at times, they would invite us to have dinner with them. It made it really nice to have such great neighbor.

After we moved, it took a couple of weeks to get used to living in a new area. When we lived in Ohio, we would get up every morning and do our chores before we ate breakfast. But our animals didn't come until a couple weeks after we moved. After they came everything had seemed to be more normal like it was before.

As summer was getting around, we were very busy. The place my parents bought only had a house on it. My parents decided to build a barn that summer for all the animals and also a place to store our hay and grain. We ended up being busy enough that we hired one of our cousins to work for us. Levi was his name. Levi was a great worker. Since we are not allowed to use electricity and everything has to be done by hand, building a barn or any kind of building takes quite a bit longer. One of the first things my father did after we moved was buy a sawmill. The sawmill was to cut our own lumber for the barn. We were building a pretty good-sized barn, and to buy all the lumber to build the barn was going to be very expensive. So buying the sawmill and cutting our own lumber was certainly going to be cheaper. Now that we had over 100 acres of wooded land, we had plenty of trees we were able to cut down and saw into lumber. However, we were not able to cut down enough trees of our own land to build the barn; not because we didn't have enough trees, it was simply because we were too busy, and we were running out of time, as we wanted the barn to be built before winter time. My father ended up having to buy quite a few logs, so we would have enough lumber to build the barn.

The first summer ended up being pretty hard, just like our cousin Menno said it would. I often thought about all my friends back in Ohio. One of the reasons that made things so hard was because we didn't know anyone in the area where we lived. It was rare that we got to go visit anyone that summer. We spent most of our time staying home and working on the farm. Not only was it that we rarely got to leave the farm, we also did not have enough families living in the community to have a church. Even if we did have a church, it was only every two weeks.

During that summer, there were more Amish families who moved in our area, and by fall, time we had enough families living in the community to have a church. Some may wonder how many families it takes to have a church in a Amish community. There is not really a specific number of families that you need to have a church. After there were six different families moved in our area, the elders got together to see what each other thought about starting a church. They all agreed that there were enough families to have a church. In order to have a church in the Amish, you do need two preachers, and it just so happens that my father and one other man in the community was a preacher. The other man who was a preacher was named Naoh. Naoh only had one arm. Sometime during his younger days, his arm got cut off by pieces of farm equipment.

After we started having a church, it certainly made things a little bit easier. As time went on, the more people I got to know and the more friends I made, the less I thought about my friends back in Ohio. However, I never forgot about them. I still think about them every once in a while. The first couple years after we had moved, we would write letters back and force to each other every once in a while. Since phones were not allowed in the Amish community, this was the only way we could reach out to each other. After several years had gone by, the writing letters back and forth to each other pretty well came to an end. After writing letters for several years, you end up finding yourself not knowing what to write or you end up writing about the same stuff just in different ways. Most of the time, what we would write about was pretty much what we were doing for work or how the weather had been and how the crops were doing. At first, when we started writing back and forth to each other we did have plenty to talk about.

New York was a lot different than Ohio. There were many exciting things to talk about, such as the wooded land we had and how we would often go for a walk into the woods. Our neighbor David owned wooded land right next to our land, and sometimes we would plan on sneaking out into the woods to hang out with each other without our parents knowing about it.

But this was nothing I could not write my friends about in Ohio because my parents would always read our letters before we would put them in an envelope.

CHAPTER SEVEN
AMISH SCHOOL

WHEN WE MOVED TO NEW YORK, I had just finished seventh grade in school. One of the things I was worried about was that I was going to have to go to school one more year with a group of children that I didn't know, which was the last thing I wanted to do. I didn't want to go to school because I was shy, and I was worried that I wouldn't fit in. Not only was I worried I wouldn't fit in, I also knew there was no one my age going to the school, which was one of the reasons I thought I wouldn't fit in. We moved in the spring, and luckily, there was no schoolhouse in the community, and there was not one built that summer before school started, so all the Amish families in the community decided they would just homeschool their children that year. I was very glad to know we were going to do homeschool, and I didn't have to go to school with other children I didn't know. As far as homeschool, I wouldn't say that it was the best thing for me. I certainly didn't learn as much as I would have if I would have gone to a school.

At the time, we were busy with getting ready to build our barn. There were many days that I would not be in school. Instead, I was outside helping with getting ready to build the barn. I was 13 years old. If you are someone outside the Amish community, you may think, *How much work can someone do at the age of 13 years old?* In the Amish community, they start their children working at a very young age. Basically, if you are old enough to walk, you are pretty much old enough to start learning how to work. I can remember at the age of four years old, I was out in the field plowing with a team of horses. Of course, one of my older brothers would be out in the field as well and was driving a team in front of me. But I was still driving the team of horses all by myself. So by the time I was 13 years old, I was able to do almost as much work as an adult person does. For the Amish community, this is pretty normal to be able to do this at such a young age.

For the days I was not going to school, I would have to go out in the sawmill work with my brother Dan. Dan would be running the sawmill and cutting the logs into lumber. I was on the other end of the sawmill, carrying away the lumber. Being on the other end of the sawmill carrying away the lumber is not the easiest job. It is quite the opposite of easy. It is a very fast paced job, especially if you are by yourself.

Not only was I taking many days off from going to school, we would only do half days of school. For me, I didn't like school and would rather be outside working than being in school. I was not very smart in school anyways. At the age of 13, I felt like I had learned everything I needed to know—which was pretty much the case if I would have stayed in the community. But being that I left the community, I wish I had learned much more in school. In the community, being highly educated was not our top priority. Being that we mostly worked home on the farm, being highly educated was not needed. Reading, writing, and doing math was pretty much what we were taught in school. We didn't learn anything about history or anything about how the outside world worked.

The reason I wish I had learned more in school is because after I left the community, there were many things that I didn't know. Mostly I felt very dumb. I was always worried that I would never be able to fit in anywhere because of being so uneducated. However, I ended up being lucky enough to make many great friends after I had left the community.

When I left the community, I had no idea how to use a cellphone. You could have handed me a calculator and told me it was a cellphone, and I would have believed you. As time went on after I left, I got to know this older couple. Their names are Mark and Lorraine. I would often spend time with Mark and his family. They ended up giving me a history book, so I could read the book and learn about the world. For me, I'm not a big reader. A book has to be very interesting for me to read. There was only one book that I read through all the way. For the rest of the books that I would read, I usually didn't make it past page 20. For the history book, I didn't find it all that interesting, but I wanted to learn about the world, and so I spent quite a bit of time reading the book.

When we lived in Ohio, I enjoyed going to school only because I would get to hang out with my friends. I still remember when I was in first grade. It took me a while to make friends. One of the reasons it took me awhile to make friends was because I was very young when I started school, and I was very small for my age. Usually we would not start school until we were six years old, but my parents decided since I was going to turn six years old a couple months after the school started, it would be okay to start early. Being that I started a year early, I was also getting done a year early, which was when I was at the age of 13. We would only go to school for eight years. There was no going to college. After we were done in school, we would work for our parents until we were old enough to work for ourselves, which was the age of 21.

After I had made friends in school, I started enjoying school. We would get two breaks and a lunch break. We would go outside and play games with each other. We would often play ball games. During the wintertime was my favorite time of the year, especially when I was going to school. There was a pretty sizable hill up behind our schoolhouse, and we were allowed to bring our sled and toboggan to school. During break, we could go outside and ride our sleds down the hill. It was rare that anyone would bring their toboggan. A toboggan was just not as much fun as a sled. It was not like you could steer a toboggan like you could with a sled.

Our sled trail went right by the side of the schoolhouse. If you were not paying attention to what you were doing, it was easy to accidentally run into the schoolhouse. It was rare that anyone would run into the schoolhouse, but it did happen to me and my brother John. John was riding with me. We didn't necessarily run into the schoolhouse. There was a fence post that was right up against the schoolhouse. The post was for anyone who would come to school with their horse and buggy, so they could tie the horse up to the post. So as me and my brother were coming down the hill, there was a small bump in the trail. As we hit the bump, it kind of distracted me, and we ran right into the fence post. We had both been sitting on the sled. The sleds that we had were set up in the front, so you could steer them. You could either lay on the sled, which is what we mostly did when we were riding along. If there was more than one person on the sled, we would sit on the sled, which is just what me and John were doing.

We were going pretty fast when we ran into the post. When we hit the post, we came to a dead stop. Me and John both when flying into the post. We both got hurt but not bad enough to where we had to go to the hospital. I remember from mostly my head hitting the post and having a pretty bad headache for the rest of the day. For my brother John, he got hurt worse than I did. He was sitting behind me. He couldn't see where we were going, and for me, right before we ran into the post, I saw that we were going to hit the post, so I had a split second to prepare myself. For my brother John not being able to see where we were going, he was not prepared. All I remember is when I was flying into the post, John came flying right over the top of me into the post. Me and John both went into the schoolhouse. John was crying pretty bad, bad enough to where I was worried for John that he may have gotten hurt badly enough he might have to go to the hospital. We had a set of stairs that went up into our schoolhouse. I was sitting on top of the stairs, and John was sitting on a bench next to the teacher. The teacher was asking John a lot of questions as to where he was hurt and if he needed to go to the hospital or if he wanted to go home. But John decided he would probably be fine staying in school for the rest of the day. Me and John both stayed inside for the rest of the day.

Luckily, that was the only time I can remember anyone having an accident during the time I was going to school. But this was not the only time someone in my family got hurt in school. It was after we had moved to New York, after the first year living in New York, the elders in the community got together and decided to build a schoolhouse. Where the schoolhouse ended up getting built was not really enough of a hill to go sliding down the hill with a sled, but there was a small brook that was right next to the schoolhouse. The brook would freeze hard enough during the winter that you could play on the ice. Most of the school children would all go out skating on the brook. Ice skates are not allowed in the community, so we would have to ice skate with whatever shoes or boots we were wearing. We would take a shovel or a broom and clear off the ice and then we would go off to the side where there was no ice and just snow. We would run toward the ice, and as we got to the ice, we would start skating. Just skating with just your boot or your shoe, you wouldn't go very far. But for my siblings and the rest of the school children going to school since they didn't have a big enough hill to ride the sled, this was the next best thing to do.

After skating day after day, they got bored doing the same thing over and over. They decided to try something different. There was a small side hill that went down toward the brook. Some of the school children got a bright idea. They had decided if they were to make a path from the top of the hill going down toward the brook, they could skate further. That was, if it was going to work. The only way that it was going to work was if they packed the snow to where it pretty well turned into ice. After packing the snow down enough, it ended up working in their favor. They would go to the top of the hill and go skating down toward the brook. For my brother Joe, it did not work out so great for him. He was skating down the hill; he lost his balance and fell over. When Joe fell over, he fell on his arm. Joe ended up breaking his wrist. He ended up having to go to the hospital.

The only doctor that in the community was a dentist. There were not many dentists in the community either. I only knew of two different dentists. When we lived in Ohio I had met one and after we moved to New York, I had met another one. Those were the only two dentists that I ever knew who were Amish. In the community, we don't go to the dentist very often. The only time we would go to the dentist was if we were having a very bad toothache. The Amish don't have very good teeth at all. A lot of the Amish end up with false teeth at some point of time in their lives. I know some who had false teeth by the time they were the age of 18. For my mother, she got false teeth when she was in her mid-40s. For the most part, if we get a toothache, we will just ride out the pain. After a while, the pain will go away. Even though the pain may go away, it might not go away forever; every once in a while, the pain would come back. After having the same teeth bother you enough times, it would come to the point where the teeth became loose enough where you could take your fingers and pull the teeth yourself. This is just what had happened to me several different times.

The Amish have bad teeth because they do not take care of their teeth. As far as brushing our teeth was concerned, it was something we would never do or use mouthwash. A lot of the Amish only go to the dentists when they barely have any teeth left. They will go to the dentists to have whatever teeth they have left taken out, so they can get false teeth. It is not against the Amish religion to brush their teeth or use mouthwash. The reason they don't brush their teeth is because they were not taught to brush their teeth as they were brought up. If they were to brush their teeth, they could certainly have much better and healthier teeth for most of their lives. However, it is just one of those things that they simply don't know about because nobody has ever brought it to their attention.

When I was in the first grade, we had a teacher that was from the Old Order Amish. The old order Amish and the Swartzentruber Amish were very different religions. The old order Amish were nowhere near as strict as the Swartzentruber Amish are. At the time, the old order Amish and the Swartzentruber Amish we were all going to the same school. The teacher from the old order Amish was very strict. Her name was Sue. If I remember, Sue only taught for half of a year. Pretty much none of the school children liked Sue. You could say Sue was very mean and angry at times. Sue would rarely ever smile, and most of us school children were scared of Sue. One day, Sue gave me and the other children in my grade a task to do. The task was to color pictures. There were five different pictures on a sheet of paper that we had to color. All five pictures on the paper were animal pictures. One of the animals in the picture was a cow. Sue told us we could color the pictures whatever color we wanted to. I decided to color the cow green. The reason I had decided to color the cow green was because we had a storybook at home. The storybook was about a farmer that had a green cow. I found the story so interesting that I always wanted to color a cow green. Sue did not like that I colored a cow green. Sue got so angry with me that she decided to give me a butt spanking because I colored a cow green. In the Amish school, the teacher has a leather belt in the desk drawer, and if we don't obey the teacher, we would get a butt spanking.

My father also had this rule, if we got a butt spanking in school, we would also get a butt spanking at home. That night, after we got home from school, one of my siblings told my parents that I got a butt spanking that day in school and why I got a butt spanking. I didn't think my father would give me a spanking, but I thought wrong. That night after dinner, my father went and got his leather belt and gave me a butt spanking. My father had a leather belt in the desk drawer at home, and if we did not obey him, he would give us a butt spanking. There were times where I disobeyed my parents and probably did deserve a butt spanking. But getting a butt spanking at the age of five years old over coloring a cow green was something I certainly did not deserve.

Sue would every once in a while give all the children in the school a task to do, and whoever did the task the best would get some kind of prize. This one day, Sue told all of us school children that if we brush our teeth the next morning before we came to school, whoever did the best job would get a gift. When we got home, we told our parents about it. Our parents didn't say much other than agreed that it would be fine if we brushed our teeth before we went to school, and so we did. When we got to school that morning, after we had all sat in our seats, Sue said that our teeth had all looked very nice. I'm not exactly sure who got the gift that morning and how she decided that person had the nicest teeth or did the best job brushing his teeth.

Sue would every once in a while ask us to brush our teeth, and we would get a gift. For about a month, she had asked us quite often to brush our teeth in order to get a gift. But after a month, Sue pretty much stopped asking us to brush our teeth. At the time, I couldn't figure out why she was pushing us to brush our teeth. I also didn't think much of it until after I left the community and I started to brush my teeth. It reminded me of the time when I was going to school, and the teacher had asked us to brush our teeth. It wasn't until then that I realized that was Sue's way of showing us that if we brush our teeth, we will have nice and healthy looking teeth. However, being that Sue didn't explain to us why she wanted us to brush our teeth, we were not going to understand. Especially not the Swartzentruber Amish. Sue was from the old order Amish, and the old order would brush their teeth. I'm guessing Sue could easily see the Swartzentruber Amish were not brushing their teeth and how bad it was for them not to brush their teeth.

The reason Sue was only a teacher for half of a year was because the teacher that we had before her was from the Swartzentruber Amish, and she had decided to leave the community. None of us school children had any idea that she was going to leave the community. We had all been at the school the same day she left. She decided to wait until that night to leave. The next morning, all of us school children went to school. When we got to the school, the teacher was not there. The school teacher was always at the school before any of the school children got there. We could not get into the schoolhouse because it was locked. The school teacher would be the one to unlock the schoolhouse. Either she would have the keys on her, or she would hide it somewhere at the schoolhouse. Either way, we had no way of getting into the schoolhouse, so we all just stood outside the schoolhouse waiting for the teacher to show up.

Sadly, the school teacher never showed up. Instead, her father showed up. His name was Andy. Andy was a great gentleman; he always seemed to be very easy going. As Andy showed up to the school you could see he had a very unhappy looking face. Andy told us that there would be no school that day. Andy said that his daughter had left the community that night, who was who was our school teacher. I do not remember what her name was. All of us school children ended up going home and told our parents what had happened. All the parents had to get together and find a teacher for the rest of the school term. It didn't take them long to find a school teacher. Only a couple of days, and we were back to school. Our new teacher was Sue.

In the Amish, it is rare that we have the same teacher for more than one year. The eight years that I went to school, there was only fifth and sixth grade that I had the same teacher. There are only between 20 to 25 children who go to the same school. Anything over 25 would be considered a big school, and the community would consider building another schoolhouse, and we would be divided up into two different schools. There was usually only one teacher, and that teacher would teach from first grade through eight years. The only time there would be more than one teacher would be if there were a lot more school children than usual. The eight years that I went to school, there only ever was one teacher.

The only other way of not having to work for your parents from the time you got done with school until you were 21 would be to leave the community. It is hardly ever that someone would leave the community just because they want to be working for themself before they reach the age of 21. The reason for someone to leave would most likely be because they do not like how strict the Amish religion is, or they do not like how strict their parents are, which is why I left. The Amish religion was already strict as it was. My father felt the need to have such strict rules for me and my siblings that it made it hard to enjoy being in the community, especially for me.

But as for the school, it took us a little while to get used to the new teacher. Sue was certainly not afraid to let us know that she was going to be a very bossy teacher right from the beginning. All of us school children were glad that we did not have sue for a teacher the following school term. I don't remember who we had for a school teacher for the next couple of years. But I do remember whoever we had was much nicer than Sue was.

When I was in the fourth grade, things turned out to be quite a bit different. As we were going to school, it was in the middle of the winter, and it was really cold outside. We woke up in the middle of the night because we could hear a lot of sirens. Living out in the country, it was rare that we would hear sirens in the middle of the night, so whenever we did hear the sirens in the middle of the night, of course, we were very curious what was going on. We would go to the window to see if we could see what was happening. This time, when we went to the window to see what was happening, we saw the schoolhouse was on fire.

When my father saw the schoolhouse was on fire, he thought it would be best if he got dressed and went to the school to see if there is anything he could help with. Some of the other neighbors around the area did the same. There was not much for my father and the rest of the neighbors that showed up for them to do. My father said they pretty well stood back and let the firefighters do their job. My father said he thought the firefighters did a very good job getting the fire out as soon as possible. However, by the time the firefighters had shown up, most of the schoolhouse was burned. The outside of the schoolhouse was built with brick. The brick walls were the only thing left standing.

For all the children who were going to that school, our elders had to either come up with a new place for us to go to school, or we were going to have to do homeschool for the rest of the school term. It didn't take the elders long to find a place where we could all go to school together for the rest of the year. There was an older Amish family who had lived right close by the schoolhouse, and they had a pretty good size buggy shop. A buggy shop in the Amish is a building where they keep their buggies when they are not using them just to keep them out of the weather. In some situations, it would also be used to store some of their farm equipment during the wintertime. The couple was an older couple and did not do much farming. Since they didn't do much for farming, they did not have a lot of farm equipment. In other words, they had plenty of room in their buggy shop. When they built the buggy shop, they made it so it could be heated during the winter time. As the elders gathered together to find a new place for the school children for the rest of the school term, they thought the older couple's buggy shop would be a great place and decided to go and ask the couple if it would be okay to use the buggy shop for the rest of the school term. The couple agreed that it would be okay.

The elders did some very quick work. It was only a couple weeks after the school had burned until we were going back to school again. Finding a place for us to go to school for the rest of the school term was not necessarily the hardest part to do. They had to get all new school books for us and new school desks. They were able to do all this in a couple of weeks and get us back to school.

Many wondered, how the schoolhouse burn? In the Amish, their schoolhouse gets heated by a wood stove. We had a small wood shed built off to the side of the school house, which is where we would store our wood for the wood stove. The teacher would bring in wood in the evening before she would go home and put it close to the stove, so the next morning, she wouldn't have to go bring wood in from the woodshed. By doing this, it would also help to dry out the wood if it was damp. Being the teacher would bring in wood and put it next to the stove, the school district just assumed that she had put the wood too close to the stove, and it caught on fire. For quite some time, we all believed this is what had happened. The school district didn't give the teacher a hard time, as they said, "We all make mistakes." Instead of giving her a hard time, the school district was very forgiving and showed their support for the teacher. Of course, when we went back to school everyone talked about the schoolhouse having burned.

As time went on things, seemed to get back to normal, and not everyone was talking about the schoolhouse being burned. As we got toward the end of the school term, the teacher asked us one morning before school started if we would like to go for a walk at lunch time to the old schoolhouse. Of course, we were all very excited to go see the old school house. It was not a very far walk, probably only a half of a mile or less.

Going to school in the Amish, we got our fair share of walking to do. We were not allowed to use a school bus. Instead, we would walk to school. The only days that we would not walk to school was when it was raining out or if it was very cold. If the temperature was not below zero, we would walk to school. For the most part, none of the school children had to walk more than a mile. Going for a half mile walk was very easy for all of us to do.

As we all walked to the old schoolhouse, all of us boys were walking in the front. The teacher and the rest of the girls were walking behind us. When we got to the old schoolhouse, there was not much there to see. The only thing that was left standing was the brick walls and part of the porch roof was still there. For the rest of the schoolhouse, the roof had all fallen in and was pretty well burned. All of us school children had gone and looked inside the school house to see what was left. But there was nothing left to see inside, as it had all been burned out. While we were there, the teacher said one of the reasons she had wanted us to come see the old school house was so we could see how dangerous fire can be.

The other reason was, right before we left, we had all been standing outside the schoolhouse, and the teacher said that she is really sorry for what had happened. She also said that she was quite certain it was her fault that the schoolhouse burned. All of us school children told the teacher that we didn't blame her for what had happened.

For the teacher to say that she was sorry meant a lot to us school children, or it did at least for me. In the Amish community, it is very rare to hear someone saying they are sorry or to hear someone say thank you. If you hear someone use either one of those words, you know they really mean it. The teacher said that she was sorry, and I could see that she had really felt bad for what had happened. For me, seeing how bad the teacher felt for what had happened, I felt bad for the teacher for what she was going through. One of the other things I remember the teacher feeling bad for was that all of the school children had built a log cabin house. We had just finished building the log cabin house several days before the school house burned.

During the wintertime, when it was too cold to go outside to play, we would just come up with games to play inside. Sometimes instead of playing games, we would build little log cabin houses, and we would put them on the corner of our desk. The log cabin houses we built looked very similar to a gingerbread house. We would take sheets of paper out of our books and roll them up. As we were rolling up the paper in order to get the paper to look like a log, we would have to take glue and put it along the end of the paper then finish rolling it up. The log cabin house was pretty well-built using glue.

After we had quite a few logs, we started building the log house, and sometimes we would even build a log barn. For this one day, some of the older school children decided to build a big log cabin house bigger than any of us had ever seen. Some of the younger children would roll up the paper into logs while the older ones were building the house. At the time I was nine years old, so I was considered more on the younger side, and I was helping roll the paper up into logs. The log house had doors and windows, and we built rooms inside the house. The log house was a two-story house. I'm not certain how long we worked on the log house; if I had to guess, we worked on it for about a month until it was done. We did not work on it every day, only when the weather was not nice enough to go outside and play. And when we did work on it, it was only when we had recess and during our lunch break. But with all of us working on it or most of us, we made pretty quick work.

When the log cabin was completely done, we had all been very proud of the log cabin house. It turned out to be just as we planned. Not only were we very proud of the log house, we were also very proud of being part of helping build it. Even the teacher thought the log house was done very well. We had a taller side book cabinet that was behind the teacher. The teacher decided to put the log cabin house on top of the cabinet, which was a great place, as all of us school children could see it while we were sitting at our desk. However, when the school house burned, so did the log cabin house. As this was also one of the things the teacher said that she felt bad about, I often thought about the log cabin house. There were times where I felt sad, knowing all the hard work we put into building the log house, and now it was gone. We never got to build another one to replace that one.

The log cabin house was not the only thing that I felt sad about. When we came to the end of the school year, everything seemed to be going very well. The family who had let us use their shop for the rest of the school year, on the last day of school, they decided to have a big lunch for us, which was very nice of them, and we were very thankful for the lunch. The food was very good. When we were done with that school term, we went home working around the home and on the farm for the summer. Just like any other year, I was very excited; we were going to have a new schoolhouse for the next term. The plan was to take down the old school house and build a new one that summer.

However, it did not turn out to be just that easy. Being that the Swartzentruber Amish and the Old Order Amish had two very different religions, they could not come to an agreement on how they wanted the new schoolhouse to be built. Taking down the old schoolhouse went just perfectly fine. When it was time to build a new school house, the Old Order Amish wanted to build the schoolhouse their way, which involved doing a lot of things that were against the Swartzentruber Amish religion, such as using power tools instead of hand tools. After the old school house was taken down, whatever was left of it, the plan was to build a new one right where the old one was. The land that the old schoolhouse was on was owned by an Old Order Amish family. Since the schoolhouse was going to be built on the land that was owned by an Old Order Amish family, the Swartzentruber Amish had really no say on how the school house was going to be built. The Old Orders had their mind set that they were going to build the school their way. Being that the Old Orders were going to build the school their way, the Swartzentruber had decided that they were not going to help them build the schoolhouse. Instead, the Swartzentruber had decided to build their own schoolhouse, and their children would no longer go to school with the Old Order Amish.

At the time I was excited to go to a new schoolhouse. But I was sad knowing that we were no longer going to school with the Old Order Amish, as I had gotten to be very close friends with several of them. After we were split up into two different schools, I never really got to see them again or hang out with them. It had often amazed me that the school district could not come to some kind of agreement, so we would all continue going to the same school and would not have to be split up into two different schools.

Since the Swartzentruber Amish were not going to help the Old Order Amish build their schoolhouse and continue going to school with them, they were left with having to find a new place to build a new schoolhouse. Some of the Swartzentruber elders in that school district got together to decide where they wanted to build a new school house; meanwhile, the Old Orders had already been well on their way with building their schoolhouse. The day came where the Swartzentruber came to an agreement where the schoolhouse would be built. It ended up being on my parents' property. The schoolhouse got built at the end of our driveway, which made it nice for me and my siblings. It was closer for us to walk to school. Being our driveway was close to half a mile long, we still had a little walk to school.

In the Amish, going to school, we would often talk about what we have been doing for work at home. As we got older, the more work we were able to do. It would make us feel like we were more of a big boy, and being a big boy would also make you look cool. Being one of the cool kids is what we all wanted to be, and by being able to do more work or being able to do what would be considered an adult kind of work made you feel like one of the cool kids. Showing up in school being able to brag about all the hard work we were able to do gave you kind of an ego, and everyone would want to be friends with you, which was what we all wanted to be. I never really got to feel like one of the cool kids. One of the reasons was because I was small for my age and also I started school a year earlier, and everyone who was in my grade was older than me. For the first couple of years, I went to school I felt very much left out, like I didn't fit in. I had always wished I was older and taller. As far as being able to do work at home, I was able to do my fair share of work even at a very young age. But I never would go to school and brag about the work I was able to do. Being that I was small for my age, I didn't think anyone would believe me. So whatever kind of work I did, I just kept it to myself.

We would get up at 5:00 in the morning. That was what time we would get up every morning unless it was Sunday morning and we did not have to go to church. Since Sunday was the day of rest in the Amish and we are not allowed to work (other than doing our chores making sure all the animals were fed), our parents would allow us to sleep in on Sunday morning. If it was a Sunday that we had to go to church, we would have to get up at 5:00, sometimes a little earlier to make sure we would get our chores done in time and not be late to church.

By sending me to school a year earlier if I passed every year, I would get done school a year earlier. In Amish school, if you don't pass a grade by the end of the school term, you will have to redo that same grade the next year. I wasn't very smart in school at all. My grade reports were usually not very good. There were several years that I only passed by a couple of points. For those couple of years, my parents were surprised that I passed. But lucky enough, I managed to pass every year. There are times where I think there had to be someone watching over me for me to not fail.

When I started school, I was getting up at 5:00 in the morning with the rest of my older siblings to help them do morning chores, which involved going out in the barn helping feed all the animals. Getting up early in the morning and going to the barn helping with the morning chores was something I enjoyed doing very much. It made me feel good, being able to get up in the morning and help with the chores; it made me feel like I somewhat fit in with the rest of the children who were in the same grade as I was. At the time, my job was to go out in the pasture and bring all the cows into the barn.

From early spring to late fall, pretty much all of our animals would be put in the pasture and then brought to the barn when we needed them. For the cows, we would bring them in every morning and in the evening to milk them. For the horses, they would not be brought to the barn every day only when we needed them.

Bringing all the cows from the pasture to the barn, that was my job every morning and in the evening. I enjoyed going to bring the cows to the barn in the evening a lot more than I did in the morning. The evening was always daylight out, and in the morning, it was always dark out. I was pretty well scared of the dark. We had two different pastures; one was for the cows, and the other one was for the horses. The pasture we had for the cows was quite a bit bigger than the one we had for the horses. The reason the one for the cows was so much bigger than the one we had for the horses was because we had a lot more cows than we did horses. All of our pasture that we had had a brook that went through the pasture, so the animals could easily go to the brook and drink water as they needed to.

The only thing I did not like about the brook was when we would get a pretty bad storm and get a lot of rain. In our cow pasture, there was a brook that ran crossways through the pasture. Sometimes the cows would cross the brook and bed down on the other side of the brook for the night. The only down part was, if the cows went across the brook to bed down for the night before we would get a bad rain storm, whenever we got a bad rain storm, the brook would rise enough where I could not go across. This would not happen very often, but it did happen every once in a while. I would have to figure out how to get across the brook and get all the cows up then get them to cross the brook. Times like this were when I was scared the most. Having to go round up all the cows early in the morning while it was black dark out and after we had just got a bad rain storm—at the age of five years old.

The first time I had to figure out how to cross the brook, I walked up and down the side of the brook to see where I could cross. The only place I could cross and it was going to be safe was crossing where the barb wire fence went across the brook. The brook went across our property into the neighbor property. The barb wire fence ran right along the property line. On our side of the property was where the cow pasture was, and on the other side the neighbor had their pasture. Going across where the barb wire fence was probably not the safest way to cross the brook, but it was the only way I could figure out how to get across the brook. I would cross by standing on the bottom of the barb wire and holding on to the top wire with my hands. I would slide across the fence until I got to the other side of the brook. When I got on the other side of the brook, I had to go round up all the cows, which was not very hard to do. I would just walk up next to the cows and say, "Get up," and they would know it was time to go to the barn. After walking up to several different cows and telling them to get up, the rest of them would start getting up without being told. I would always try to get up the older cows first, as they were the ones who would lead the way to the barn, and the younger ones would follow.

For the cows, it was much easier for them to cross the brook than it was for me. Usually they didn't have any issue crossing the brook other than for this one time, when the water had risen pretty high. The cows were having a hard time figuring out where they were going to cross. They walked up the side of the brook and turned around and walked back down the side of the brook to see where the water was shallower, so they could cross. After walking up and down the side of the brook one of the older cows found a spot to cross where it was not quite as deep, but it was still deep. I remember seeing the water to be well over their knees.

After all the cows crossed the brook, now I had to go back across the brook, which met to go cross by the barb wire fence. By the time I had gotten across the barbed wire fence, the cows were well on their way to the barn. Once I crossed the brook, I took off running till I caught up to the cows. Before I had caught up to them, I was very scared. But once I caught up to them, I no longer was scared. On a morning like this, when I got all the cows to the barn, I was glad that it was over and had hoped next time would be much easier.

We had a dog named Sport. He would often go with me to get the cows, which made me feel much safer. But, of course, on a morning like this Sport had no interest in going with me to get the cows. Instead, he would just stay in the barn.

Going to get the cows early in the morning when it was black dark out, I had known I was going to be scared until I found the cows, but after that, I was fine. But I was not going to say a word to anyone that I was scared. The reason was, it made me feel like I was more of a big boy, and it was about the only thing I was doing at the time that made me feel like I was a big boy.

As fall came around and it was going to be my first year going to school, for the first couple of weeks after the school started, my mother was perfectly fine with me getting up early in the morning to go help doing the morning chores, or if she wasn't, she just didn't say anything. After a couple of weeks, my mother decided that it was too much for me at such a young age to get up so early in the morning to help do the morning chores and then go to school all day. So my mother asked me to stay in bed for an extra hour in the morning and not get up to help with the morning chores. I was very upset that my mother had asked me to stay in bed for an extra hour in the morning. I was worried if the other children in my grade found out I had to stay an extra hour in bed in the morning they would pick on me for not being a big boy. Luckily, they never found out; and if they did, they never said a word to me.

I would lay in bed and listen to my older siblings getting up to go do morning chores. I had wished I could get up and go help do morning only because it made me feel like a big boy. I do remember thinking to myself that I was glad that I no longer had to go get the cows in the dark. For me, lying in bed listening to my older sibling getting up in the morning, I would never be able to fall back asleep. After a couple of months going by listening to my older siblings getting up to go do morning chores and me not being able to fall back asleep, I had decided to tell my mother that I was not able to fall asleep after my older sibling got up. My mother didn't really respond to what I said. So I decided to start getting up early in the morning and go help my older sibling do chores and see if my mother was going to say anything. My mother never said a word to me, so from there on I continue getting up early in the morning.

CHAPTER EIGHT
WORKING FOR ANOTHER AMISH FAMILY

AS FAR AS WORKING FOR ANOTHER AMISH FAMILY was something me and my sibling rarely ever did, especially not when we lived in Ohio, as we had plenty of work for ourself. After we moved to New York, there was this one family we had thought very highly of. They lived about three miles from us. His name is Jacob. Jacob and his family were one of the most respected Amish families I had ever met. Jacob was a very smart man; you could learn a lot from him just by working with him. Jacob was the type of person who would never judge a person for who they are or for what they do. Jacob was also not someone that would get jealous of what someone else would have going for themself. He would mind his own business and not worry about what someone else is doing. He was not the type that would try to cause trouble in the community; the last thing he wanted to do was to cause trouble in the community.

I always thought that Jacob would be a very good leader in a community.

Shortly after I had turned the age of 14, Jacob stopped by our house one evening. He had stopped by to ask my father if one of us boys could do chores for him. He and his wife and some of their younger children had decided to go to Ohio to visit some of their families and needed someone to feed their animals while they were gone. My father decided it would be okay for one of us to do his chores while they went to Ohio to visit their family.

My father decided to send me to do his chores. I would have to go there in the evening to the chores and spend the night at Jacob's house, so I would be there to do the chores the next morning. Jacob and his wife were leaving to go to Ohio early on a Thursday morning, so Jacob had me come over to their place on a Wednesday afternoon, so he could show me how to do the chores. This was the first time I had ever worked for another Amish family. Not only was the first time I worked for another Amish family, it was also the first time my father allowed me or one of my siblings to work for another Amish family. Being I was going to be the first one in our family to work for another Amish family, I was very nervous. I was worried that I would not be able to do all of Jacob's chores and do a good job at it.

Jacob showed me how to do some of the chores, and for the rest, he told me how to do them. At the time, I was very slow minded and not very quick to pick up on things. There was a lot of stuff that Jacob told me how to do, and I just simply didn't understand him. The chores that he showed me how to do, I was perfectly fine with doing them and understanding how he wanted them to be done. Most of the chores that I didn't understand how to do were the morning chores.

Jacob had around 48 calves to feed and around 10 horses, three cows, and several pigs. Of course, I didn't have to do the chores all by myself. But it was my responsibility to make sure they all got done and were done right. Jacob's oldest son was old enough to help with doing some of the chores. His name is Amos. Amos had two sisters who were older than him, but they mostly helped with the work in the house. The two sisters were not the only siblings Amos had. I'm not exactly sure how many children Jacob's family had at the time; if I had guessed it was probably around eight at the time.

They were also going to school at the time and would have to sleep in in the morning, so they would not get tired while they were in school. The schoolhouse where they were going was four to five miles away, which was too far to walk, so they had to use a horse and buggy to get there, which was also one of my responsibilities; to make sure the horse was hitched to the buggy and ready for them to go to school on time. I always made sure the horse was hitched to the buggy and ready to go in plenty of time. The last thing I wanted was for Jacob's children to be late for school. I knew if they were late for school, I was going to get the blamed for it, which would not look good for me.

Not only did Jacob and his wife need someone to do the chores in the barn, they also needed someone to take care of the house while they were gone. There was another Amish family who lived right close by my us. Their name was David Salchbaugh, but I cannot remember what David's wife's name is (which shouldn't be that hard to remember because of the five years that I was living at home after we moved to New York). We lived right next to them and went to church with David and his family and often went to their place. Remembering names is something I have always struggled with. David and his wife had quite a few girls in their family, and when another family needed help with doing stuff around the house, they would often lean more toward David's family to ask them for help, which is just what Jacob and his wife did.

The same evening Jacob and his wife came to my parents to ask for one of us boys to do his chores, it was also the evening they went to David's family to ask them if they could hire one of their daughters to take care of the house while they were gone. David and his wife agreed that one of their girls could take care of the house while they were gone. David and his wife have a daughter named Fanny. They had decided Fanny would be able to take care of Jacob's family house while they were gone. Fanny would also go there in the afternoon toward the evening and spend the night at Jacob's house. Fanny would go home during the day. Since nobody was going to be at Jacob's house during the day, there was nothing for her to do. Jacob's children who were going to school had to drive right by our house and also drove right by Fanny's home on their way to school. Being that Jacob's children were going right by Fanny's family's place on their way to school, she would just get a ride with them and get dropped off at her place. Fanny and her family also had to babysit some of Jacob's children. Jacob's children who were not old enough to go to school and did not go to Ohio with their parents needed to be babysit while Jacob's and his wife were gone to Ohio. So Fanny and her family agreed that they would babysit Jacob's children until they got back. Since me and Fanny were going to Jacob's in the afternoon, instead of both of us driving there, Fanny would walk to our house and then we would ride together. In the Amish the man is always the one doing the driving. You will never see a married Amish couple driving down the road where the woman is driving. However, the woman does get to drive quite often. It is often that the woman will go to town or go shopping by themself. For me and Fanny riding together going to Jacob's, once we got there, she didn't have to worry about unhitching the horses from the buggy. When we got to Jacob's, she would go in the house and start doing her work that she needed to do in the house.

As for me, I would unhitch the horse and bring the horse to the barn; after that, I would start doing the evening chores. Jacob's son Amos was around the age of 10 years old, which was plenty old enough to help with the chores. We would start doing the chores until it was supper time. Usually one of the younger children, who was in the house helped Fanny do house work and also helped with the cooking would come out and tell us when super was ready. We all gathered around the table to eat. There was not much talking at the supper table. We didn't know each other very well, so there was just not much for us to talk about.

After supper was done, I went to the barn and continued with the chores. Amos would spend time in the house for a while before he would come to the barn to help with the chores. Fanny and the rest of the children would also come out to the barn to help with the chores after they got done cleaning up the supper table all cleaned all the dishes. Fanny would help with milking the cows and feeding all the calves in the evenings. In the morning, she only helped with milking the cows, as she had a lot more house work to do in the morning than she did in the evening. She would cook dinner for everyone in the evening and also cook breakfast for everyone in the morning. But not only was she cooking breakfast for everyone in the morning, she also had to make lunch for all the children who were going to school. As I'm not exactly sure what she was making for their lunches, but I imagine it was something pretty simple. At the time, Jacob and his wife had four children going to school. Packing four lunch pails may not seem like it would take a long time, and it probably didn't, but by the time she had all the dishes clean, packed the lunch pails, and made sure everyone was dressed and ready to go in time, she'd done plenty of work.

For me, I didn't have to push in the morning to get my chores done as long; as I had a horse hitched to the buggy in time for them to go to school, I was all set. As time went on, I got to be very good at doing the chores. The one thing that took a while to do was milking the cows. Two out of the three cows that we had to milk were in their prime time, meaning they were giving a lot of milk, and it took quite a while to milk them. If a cow is in their prime time, they can easily fill a five-gallon bucket. Since we were not allowed to have electricity, we have to milk the cows by hand. Milking a cow by hand that fills a five-gallon pail will take close to half an hour. Luckily for me, I didn't have to milk all three cows by myself. I was glad Fanny helped milking the cows. Fanny was a really fast milker, which was a big help.

Jacob and his wife were gone to Ohio for almost two weeks. For the first several days, it was taking me quite a while to do the chores. However, once I got used to doing the chores, I got to be pretty fast at it. I would try to cut corners as much as I could to get the chores done quicker. One morning, cutting corners and getting the chores done earlier did not work out so good for me. Jacob had a small wagon you easily pulled by hand. Almost all Amish have a small wagon like this. The wagon was for us to use around our home. I got this bright idea, or I thought it was a bright idea, to take the wagon and put it right behind the cows and put two milk cans on the wagon. Putting two milk cans next to each other was pretty much all you could get on the wagon. I got the idea that if I put the two milk cans on the wagon and put it right behind the cows, when we got done milking the cows or the pail would fill up, we would just dump the milk from the pail into the milk can. One milk can would hold 10 gallons.

Milking the cows and dumping the milk from the pail into the milk can went perfectly fine. My idea was once we are done milking, I would just pull the wagon to the milk house instead of carrying the pail to the milk house every time it filled up the pail. How much time was I saving by doing this? Not enough to make a difference maybe a couple of minutes at the most. When I went to bring the milk on the wagon into the milk house the wagon ended up tipping over, and the milk dumped out of the cans all over the barn floor. The reason the wagon tipped over was because going around the corner to go into the milk house was very tight. I ended up having to back the wagon up to make a bigger loop to make it into the milk house. The corner was hard to make because of the barn gutter. In order for me to make it into the milk I had to get as close to the barn gutter as I could. As I was backing the wagon getting as close to the gutter as I could to make a bigger loop to go into the milk house, I accidentally got too close to the gutter, and that is how the wagon tipped over.

The milk was brought into the milk house and put in cold water, so it would not go bad. In a Amish milk house, there is a hold dug into the ground around three feet deep and three feet wide and roughly eight to 10 feet long. After the hole was all dug out, the bottom and the side would be poured with concrete roughly three inches thick.

Basically, it was a big concrete tank that sat in the ground and would get filled up with cold water. The concrete tank was called a "cistern." After the Cistern was filled with cold water, we would put the can with milk into the water. This was how we would keep the milk from going bad. If you had food that you wanted to keep from going bad for a couple of days, the cistern could easily be us for that, too.

The worst part about having the milk dumped on the barn floor was that the milk was getting used to feed some of the calves. The milk would be brought in the house and would get warmed up on the stove and then we would have to bring it out to the barn and feed it to the calves. The milk that we would get in the morning would be used in the evening and the milk that we got in the evening would be used in the morning. As the milk that I had dumped on the flour was in the morning, now we didn't have milk to feed to the calves that evening. When that evening came around, we had to wait until we had milked one of the cows, so we could bring the milk into the house and start warming it up. Bringing the milk into the house and having it warm up was one of the first things we would do; it would take a little while for it to warm up. However, on this evening, that was not the case. Not only were we not able to bring the milk in and get it warmed up so the calves would not get fed too late, we also were not able to feed the calves as much milk that night as we usually would. We had to keep some of the milk for the next morning to feed them.

That evening, when I went to bed, all I could hope was that the calves were going to be fine; being they got fed less milk that evening than they usually would, I was worried. The next morning when I woke up, the first thing I did when I got in the barn was check on the calves and make sure they were all doing fine. Luckily, the calves were all doing great. Seeing that the calves were all doing good definitely made me feel much better. However, the next day when I got to Jacob's to do his chores, I noticed one of the calves was sick. I started getting very worried, as I had no idea what I was going to do.

Most of the Amish have some kind of medicine in the barn to give it to their animal when they don't feel good or are sick. I started looking around Jacob's barn for medicine to give it to the calf, but I had no luck finding any medicine to give to the calf. So I continued doing the chores until it was suppertime. After we got done eating supper, I went to the barn to do the rest of the chores as some of Jacob's children came out to help do the chores as well. When Fanny got to the barn, I told her that one of the calves was sick, and I had no idea what to give the calves to make it feel better. Fanny decided to just give the calve warm milk and that would be all we would give the calf that evening.

I had my mind so much on the calf that I forgot to feed the pigs that night. It wasn't until after we had all gone to bed until I realized I did not feed the pigs. I lay in bed thinking if I should get up and go feed the pigs or just wait until the morning to feed them. After laying there thinking for a while I decided I was going to wait to feed them until the morning. It was pretty late in the night, and part of me would simply be too scared to get up during the night to go feed the pigs. However, between the calf not feeling good and the pigs not getting fed, I did not get very much sleep that night. When the next morning came around, the first thing I did was go check on the calf and then feed the pigs. The pigs I had known, other than being really hungry, were going to be fine; I was worried that the calf might not be alive anymore. As I walked into the barn, I checked on the calf and came to a surprise the calf was perfectly fine. After seeing the calf was doing fine, I hurried up and went to give the pigs some food. I would always wait to feed the pigs until last, but this morning I decided to give them some food first thing in the morning, then when I was done doing all the rest of the chores, I would feed them again which is just what I did.

For the calf, one of the reasons I was surprised seeing that it was doing perfectly fine was because it was very cool. The temperature was well below zero that morning, and it was pretty cool in the barn. Being that it was very cool, it is sometimes hard for a sick calf to get better without giving medicine. Luckily the warm milk worked in our favor.

As the next several days went by, everything seemed to be going perfectly fine or the way thing should be going. As I woke up one morning, I was taking my time getting dressed to go in the barn to the chores, not being in any hurry to go to the barn as I didn't have a reason to be in a hurry. When I got to the barn started doing the chores, I happened to notice that two calves were missing. One of the first days I started doing the chores, I counted all the calves, as I was just curious to know how many calves Jacob had. When I counted the calves, I got 48, and I counted them twice to make sure I didn't miss count. Both times, I got 48. This morning when I realized that there were two calves missing, I counted them again and I counted them several times. Every time I counted them, I only got 46. The last time I counted them, I knew for sure that there were two calves missing. I started looking everywhere in the barn, as I thought they may have gotten lost and are somewhere in the barn. After looking everywhere in the barn, the calves were nowhere to be found in the barn, so I thought maybe they somehow got out of the barn and were somewhere on the outside of the barn.

We had just got several inches of snow that night, so if they got out of the barn, it should be easy to find them just by their track. I walked around the whole outside of the barn. I didn't see any track at all, nor did I see any sign of the calves. After looking everywhere for the calves and not finding them anywhere, I started to think maybe someone came and stole a couple of them in the middle of the night. But then again, if someone did come and steal a couple of calves in the middle of the night, I would have been able to see the track in the snow. Being that I didn't see any tracks or have any idea what could have happened to the calves, I had no idea what to do. After giving up hope that I would find the calves, I had decided not to tell a word to anyone about the missing calves. I was very worried when Jacob got home, he would definitely realize that there are a couple of the calves missing. Part of me kept thinking, *Maybe he won't notice…* or at least that is what I was hoping.

The last couple of days that I was doing the chores, everything went very well. But being with everything that had gone wrong and with the calves going missing, I was worried that if Jacob noticed the calves had gone missing, he would complain to my father that I did not do a very good job doing the chores and would never want to hire me again. I had known if Jacob didn't think that I did a very good job there would be talk in the community about me not being a very good hired hand. As I had felt sad for a couple of days, as I was afraid this was excellent what was going to happen.

In the Amish, it is very hard to work for another Amish family without them complaining about your help. Not only is it hard working for another Amish family, you also don't make a lot of money. At the time the pay was only $12 to $15 a day. Working for another Amish family and getting paid $15 a day is considered very good pay. When the Amish work outside the community, they certainly make quite a bit more. A lot of the Amish families have a very hard time finding someone to work for them because of not good pay, and it is hard work for another family when they are not happy with the work you did for them.

I think this was one of the reasons my father rarely had me or one of my siblings working for another Amish family. Jacob's family was the only Amish family that my father would let us work for. After Jacob and his wife got home from the trip, it was about a week until Jacob came to pay my father for the work I had done. Since I wasn't the age of 21 and was not allowed to have any money for myself, Jacob had to pay my father. I also have no idea what my father charged Jacob for the work I had done. I imagine it was not very much. After Jacob left our place to go back home, I was worried that my father was going to call me to the house or ask me to stay in after we got done eating supper that evening. As I was quite certain that Jacob was going to be very disappointed with the work I had done. Of course, if Jacob was going to be disappointed with the work I had done, my father wasn't going to be very happy with me, and like most things, if my father wasn't very happy with the work I had done, it would lead to some kind of punishment as this was my biggest fear.

A couple days went by, and my father hadn't said a word of what Jacob thought of the work I had done. Then this one we were sitting at supper table eating and everybody was pretty quiet. All of the sudden, my father said, "The other day when Jacob was here, he said that he was very happy with the work you have done."

I didn't really say anything. All I remember was thinking how surprised I was to hear those words. From what I can remember, this was the first time I had anyone say that I had done good work, and they were happy with the work I had done. I had felt very proud of myself. This was also not the only time I worked for Jacob's family. Every once in a while, Jacob would stop by our place and ask if I could work for him for several days or for a week. For the most part, my father would always tell Jacob that I could work for him, and I had always looked forward to working for Jacob and his family.

At the time, when I was working for Jacob, it was mostly during the wintertime. The work that we were doing was cutting firewood. The Amish do not believe in using electric or propane to heat their house. We would only use wood or coal. When we lived in Ohio, we had used quite a bit of coal because we did not have access to firewood like we did after we moved to New York. Pretty much all of the Amish in New York had plenty of firewood on their land. Since there was not much to do during the wintertime, cutting firewood was something that would keep us busy. The reason Jacob needed help cutting firewood was because all his children who were old enough to help with doing that kind of work were going to school. Cutting firewood is something you need two people to do. Being that a chainsaw was not allowed to be used, we had to cut our firewood by hand. The saw that we would use was called a crosscut saw. The crosscut saw was anywhere from five to seven feet long. The saw had a handle on each end of it. One person would stand on each end of the saw, and pulling the saw back and forth is how the wood is cut. Cutting firewood during the winter time, there were a lot of days that it was very cold, but because of using a saw like this to cut our wood we always stay warm.

Being that Jacob only needed me during the day, I would drive to their place in the morning and then drive back home in the evening. On the days that it was really cold, Jacob's wife would make me a cup of hot chocolate for the ride home. I always thought it was really nice for Jacob's wife to make me a cup of hot chocolate. The hot chocolate was always very delicious.

Sometime after I left the community, I had heard that Jacob and his family had appreciated all the work I had done for them. I had also heard that Jacob thought I was a very good worker. Jacob also said that he thought I would be someone his kids could look up to in the future. But being that I left the community, Jacob said the one thing he hoped his kids would never do was follow my footsteps and leave the community. Hearing that Jacob thought I was a very good worker and someone his kids could look up to in the future made me feel really good, as I had thought very highly of Jacob. However, I understood why Jacob would not want his children to follow my footsteps and leave the community.

As for myself, I hope Jacob's children enjoy living the Amish life enough to where they don't want to leave the community. Certainly I wouldn't wish for Jacob's children or for anyone's children to get made fun of to the point where they can no longer enjoy the life they want to live.

After I had left the community. the one question I often got was, what life do I enjoy most: living the English life or living the Amish life? For a lot of people who have left the community ended up not liking the outside life at all. But some of the people who have left the community end up liking the outside life better. If you are someone who likes living the Amish life, and you feel like you fit in or you have friends you enjoy hanging out with, but you decide to leave the community simply because you are interested in experiencing the outside life, it is most likely you will end up not liking the outside life and will end up returning to the community. However, if you are someone who leaves because you didn't feel like you fit in or were getting picked on for what you wear or the way you look and your father had very strict rules, it is most likely that you will end up enjoying the outside life over the Amish life, which was just what had happened for me.

For me, after I left, I felt relief from fear. It was a fear of when was the next time my father was going to be angry with me or give me a butt spanking for no reason. Or was he going to make up another rule that would make me fit in less than I already did? Other things I also feared were when we were working in the fields, was anything that broke on the equipment? Or if something broke on the harness the horse had on, my father would often get very upset and angry, and he was not afraid to do his fair share of yelling at us. Sometimes his yelling got bad enough that I thought he was going to give me a butt spanking over something that was worn-out to the point where it simply could not hold up anymore. These are just some of the things I no longer had to fear after I left.

Living the English life and away from your family isn't all that fun; there're many nights you lie in bed thinking about your family, wishing things could have worked out. But after I left, I knew there was a reason that I left. Going back to living the same Amish religion as my family is simply not going to work. I would not be able to enjoy the life that I'm living knowing everyone in the community was going to look down on me for what I had done.

The one thing that helped me a lot living the English life was my grandfather on my dad's side. His name was Harvey. I never got to see my grandfather Harvey after I left. Several months before I left, my uncle, Dan, was building a barn. My father decided to send me and my brother John to help them for a day. Uncle Dan's had taken over my grandfather's farm. When me and my brother John arrived at Uncle Dan's place, I decided to go visit my grandfather before I started work for the day (plus the weather was not very nice out, so visiting my grandfather was going to be more fun). My grandfather and I talked for quite a while. It was one of the best visits I ever had with my grandfather. For my grandmother on my dad's side, I don't know what her name was. We would always just call her grandma. For as long as I can remember, my grandma was not doing very well. She was in the wheelchair for a long time. I can't ever remember seeing her walk. It was also not very easy to carry on a conversation with her. She had a hard time hearing and might not be able to understand what you are saying.

As I was visiting my grandfather, he told me that Grandma was doing better than she had in a long time. I remember just hearing my grandfather saying that it had made me feel really good. I could see that my grandfather was also doing really well. He seemed to be very happy. My grandfather was not doing well enough that he could go outside and work though. He mainly stayed in the house. For me to go visit him, I'm sure he was glad that I did go visit him just to give him something to do. He had a bird feeder outside the window. He told me that in the morning, he would sit there and watch the birds. This was a way to give him something to do. It seemed like he liked to watch the birds come and feed off the bird feeder.

I don't remember exactly what me and my grandfather talked about that day. My grandfather would read the Bible a lot, as I can remember one of the things that he told me was how important it is to read the Bible. My grandfather had also been a bishop in his church district. He was a bishop as long as I can remember, so reading the Bible was something he did a lot.

After I got done visiting my grandfather and went back out to work, most of the day, I thought of my grandfather and how glad I was that I went and visited. Even after I left the community, I would often think about my grandfather. I had often wondered what he thought of me when he found out that I left the community. When I left the community, my grandfather was one of the people I felt I had let down the most, as I was quite certain he was very disappointed in me. It bothered me a lot knowing that could very well be the case. I hoped if one person could forgive me for what I had done, it would be my grandfather. After that last visit with my grandfather, I thought very highly of him.

Chapter Nine

Amish Funeral

S EVERAL MONTHS AFTER I HAD LEFT, I found out that both my grandfather and my grandmother had passed away. They both passed within a couple weeks from each other. My grandma passed away first, and about two weeks after my grandfather passed away. It wasn't until several days after my grandfather's funeral that I found out that they both passed away. It was not surprising to hear that grandma passed away because she had not been doing good for many years. But to hear that my grandfather passed away was very surprising to me, as I thought my grandfather was still doing very well.

For the next couple of weeks, I thought of my grandfather a lot. There have been many times where I was very undecided the way I'm living my life is the right choice. However, at the end of the day, something told me that I was on the right path. Times like this, it seemed like someone was watching over me, and I often thought between God and my grandfather, they would guide me in the right direction. It was also hard for me not being able to go to my grandfather's funeral, as I had wish I could have seen him one last time. But at the same time, it was also good to know the last time I had seen him was one of the best times I had spent with him.

This was also not the only time that I had enjoyed spending time with him. When we still live in Ohio, he would come and visit us every once in a while. Every time he would come to visit us, he would always have some kind of treat for us. Most of the time, it would be a piece of candy. When we were living in Ohio, we were milking enough cows to be shipping milk, meaning we were milking enough cows for a milk truck to come pick up our milk and take it to a milk factory, which was around 10 to 12 cows that we were milking. Having to milk only 10 to 12 cows doesn't seem like it would take a long time, but being that we had to milk them by hand, it would take quite a while. There were usually four or five of us who would sit down to milk cows along with our parents, and it would take anywhere from one hour to an hour and half. After my mother and father had gone to the barn to help milking the cows, me and my sister Mary got to stay in the house with our grandfather Harvey.

I remember he was reading the Bible to us. He would read some and then he would explain to us what exactly had happened. I also remember being very much interested in what he was reading, as I thought it was very exciting to listen to him read. After he got done reading to us before our parents came in from the barn, he gave me and my sister Mary each a piece of candy. I felt really happy and excited to get a piece of candy. After he had passed away, I often thought of all the great times I had spent with him. Finding out that both of my grandparents passed away several days after the funeral had bothered me a lot, as I knew my relationship with my family and the rest and the rest of Amish was not very good. But I was surprised that no one in the Amish community let me know, so if I wanted to, I could have gone to the funeral.

It is not the first time someone in the Amish community had left and someone in their family ended up passing away or someone in their family would get married, and the family would end up inviting them home during that time. But that was certainly not the case for me. The only time I was invited back home was to rejoin the community. Since I had felt that I was pushed out of the community, rejoining was just not going to happen. Would I have gone to my grandfather's funeral if I would have been invited? Probably not. But it would have made me feel good and would have let me know my family and the rest of the community was thinking of me. Why I was not invited to come home during that time, I have no idea, other than my father just being very strict. He didn't want me to come home during that time simply because it may not have made him look as strict as he wanted the community to see him as.

As far as going to a funeral is concerned, it was not something that I liked doing. Seeing a person laying there and no longer being alive would often make me very lightheaded to the point where I felt like I was going to pass out. During the time that I was still in the community, I only went to two different funerals. One of them was when I was around the age of six years old. The funeral was for my grandfather on my mother's side. His name was Danny. Danny was not doing very well for a long time or as long as I could remember. He spent a lot of time in the wheelchair. But Danny was very good with carrying on conversation, and as long as I can remember, he never lost his memory. He was very good at remembering your name and recognizing who you are. But the time came where his health condition got a lot worse, and he ended up passing away. The other time I was to a funeral in the Amish was after we had moved to New York. Our neighbor David had a child who was often very sick and had to go to the doctor quite often. As I'm not sure what the child had, he kept getting sick. Whatever it was, it was something the doctor couldn't help much with. The child's parents had even made up their own kind of medicine that was helping him some. The parents tried everything they could. But with the doctors not being able to help much, the day came where the child could no longer survive and passed away.

It is a very hard and sad day for a lot of the Amish to see a child pass away. The Amish community likes to see everyone do good health-wise and live until they are old. But just like the outside world, it does not always happen. I also went to several different funerals after I had left the community. One of the things that I was surprised by was how the Amish and the English funerals are done very similar to each other, just in different ways.

The Amish funerals are certainly not nearly as expensive as the English funerals are. The Amish will make their own coffin which is made out of wood. The coffin is most likely made by someone in the community who is good with making furniture, and it is made very well. They are made out of finished lumber, and after the coffin is made, they will give the coffin a dark varnish. They also have a rough box that is also made out of wood. The rough box is built pretty strong but does not look very fancy. The only really expense the family has is paying the guy who made the coffin; otherwise, it doesn't cost them anything to have the funeral. They have the funeral at their house, so it's not like they have to pay someone to do the funeral. Most of this may seem very different from an English funeral.

But the part that is very similar is, the day of the funeral everyone who is coming to the funeral will gather together in the morning at the family's place. There will be some singing and preaching, but it does not last as long as going to church does. Once they are done singing and preaching, everyone will walk by the coffin to get to see the person one last time. After everyone walks by the coffin one last time, they will then close up the coffin and the preacher will preach for several more minutes. When he gets done preaching, everyone will go to the cemetery. The Amish community does have their own cemetery. The buggy that brings the coffin to the cemetery will be the first one to leave the driveway, and the rest of the buggies will follow.

Once they get to the cemetery, there will be two pieces of wood over the hole that is dug in the ground, and the coffin will be placed on top of the wood. Once the coffin is placed on top of the wood, everyone will gather around the coffin. After everyone is gathered around the coffin, they will sing a couple different songs, and the preacher will again preach for a short period of time. Once they are done singing and preaching, the coffin will be placed in the hole by the pallbearers. Then the pallbearers will start filling in the hole with shovels.

The one thing I noticed that was different was in the English funerals the pallbearers are usually someone who is related to the person that passed away. In the Amish, there are four people chosen to be pallbearers. Those four people are someone outside the family and not related to them. Once the pallbearers start filling in the hole you can stay and watch them fill in the hole if you want to. Otherwise, you start heading back to the family house, which is where everyone goes once they are done at the cemetery and where they gather together to have a meal. When we would gather together to have a meal at an Amish funeral, instead of sitting at the table we would stand around the table, and as for food, it would be a pretty simple meal.

As I don't remember exactly what we would have, but I do remember that we would have bread and jam, and there were also canned pickles and canned beets. That was pretty much the main meal. Most likely if you have a meal at an Amish funeral, you will be hungry by the time you get home. However, I'm sure worrying about making sure everyone gets enough to eat on the day of the funeral is probably one of the last things most people are thinking. The reason the pallbearers were someone who was not related to the family was because in the Amish when someone passes away, the family is not allowed to do any work until after the funeral. Any work that needs to be done around the house or feeding their animals would be done by someone else in the community, and it cannot be someone related to the family. Being a pallbearer does involve working, like digging the grave and then filling it back in, and this is why the pallbearers had to be outside the family and not related to family.

One of the funerals I went to after I left was Carl's funeral. It was a surprise for me when I heard that Carl passed away. I had known Carl had some health issues, but as far as I knew, he was still doing very well.

After finding out that he had passed away, one of the first things that came to mind was the night I had left the community and stayed at his house for several days. As I thought to myself, *I would have no idea where else I would have gone if it hadn't been for Carl...* It made me sad knowing he had passed away. I decided I was going to the wake and funeral. My first thought was that it was probably going to be very different from an Amish wake and funerals, but it turned out everything seemed to be done pretty much the same way.

In the Amish funerals, when we got done eating lunch, we would hang out at the family's place for a bit longer before we would go home. For all the boys, they would go hang out in the barn, and for the men, they would hang out by the house. Some of the men may be hanging out in the living room, and for the other men, they would hang out on the porch. For all the boys who would go hang out in the barn, a lot of the boys would always get into some kind of trouble. Most of the time, it was not that they were getting into trouble in a bad way they were just being boys.

At my grandfather's funeral on my mother's side, several of the boys got into a very bad fight. I don't remember what exactly had happened that led to such a bad fight. One of those boys was my brother Dan. Dan and one of his friends got into a fight with several of the boys who were much younger than they were. From what I had heard, Dan and his friends took the fight way too far. Before we left the funeral to go home, my father had already found out about Dan getting into a fight, and he was very upset with Dan for getting into a bad fight at our grandfather's funeral. That evening before we went to bed, my father asked Dan why he and his friend had decided to get into a bad fight. Dan did not have a good answer of why he and his friend decided to get into a fight with several other boys who were much younger than they were. My father was so angry with Dan that he decided that kind of behaviorwas not acceptable. My father went to his desk and got his leather belt out and made Dan bend over a chair, and my father gave Dan a butt spanking in front of the whole family. There were times where my father gave us butt spanking that was very unnecessary, but if Dan and his friend got into a bad fight with several boys much younger than they were for no reason, it was most likely that they both did deserve a butt spanking.

Dan was the type of person who got in trouble quite often. You could say he was a wild child. When Dan was 17, one Sunday morning, we had to go to church. He decided to pretend he was sick, so he didn't have to go. This was something there would be no way I would be able to pull off, but for Dan, he was. He got up in the morning with the rest of us, when he came down the stairs, he told my mother he was very sick and would not even be able to go help with the morning chores. My mother told him he should probably just go back to bed, so he did. We all believed that he was very sick and would not be able to go to church. My father decided I should stay home with Dan, so he wouldn't be by himself all day. About an hour after everyone left, Dan got up and went outside. I was upstairs lying in bed, and when he went outside I thought he was just going to the barn to go to the bathroom. After an hour went by Dan and still hadn't come back in, I started to get worried, so I went downstairs in the kitchen where I could see out to the barn to see if I could see him. I did not see him anywhere. I hung out in the kitchen for another hour, and I kept looking out the window. Another whole hour went by, and he was nowhere to be seen. By this time, I was worried enough; I thought maybe something happened to him. I put on my hat and boots and went to the barn. I looked everywhere for him and even yelled his name several times, but there was still no sign of him. I went back in the house until it was close to lunchtime, then I went back out to feed the animals. Most of the animals were out in the pasture. It was just mainly the chickens that I fed and gathered the eggs. I thought for sure by the time I would get back to the house, Dan would have back from wherever he went.

Lunchtime came, and Dan was still nowhere to be found. I was so worried, I don't think I even ate lunch that day. It was getting to be midafternoon, and there was still no sign of him. I started to think he most likely left the Amish that day. It certainly would not have surprised me if he did, being he was a wild child. I thought I was going to have to tell my parents when they got home from church, "He left the house this morning and hasn't come back."

It was almost 3:00. I was sitting in the living room, thinking my parents and the rest of my siblings were going to be home from church anytime. All of the sudden, I heard the house door open and then close. I went to see who it was, and it was Dan. He took off his boots and went upstairs. He told me not to say a word to anyone. To this day, I still haven't said a word to anyone. I often wonder where he went.

One of the questions I often got after I had left the community was, what would happen if someone left the community, and they had some kind of an accident that they ended up passing away? What would happen with his or her body? When we lived in Ohio, this was something that did happen every once in a while, but it wasn't something that happened very often. You would hear of quite a lot of accidents that would happen from Amish teens who had left the community. But most of them walked away with just a few bruises. In a situation where someone who had left the community and had some kind of accident that he or she passed away, they would be brought back home to their parents place and were buried in the Amish community.

For this one Amish man named Sam Hershberger, he did leave Amish community when he was a teenager. He had left for about five years before he decided to go back to the Amish. There were many stories that we heard about Sam that he was quite the trouble maker, such as trying to outrun the police, and from what we had heard, there were several times that he was successful doing so.

The day came where Sam no longer enjoyed living the English life and decided to return to the Amish community. Sam ended up getting a girlfriend after he returned to the community, and eventually, he got married. Sometime after they got married, Sam became a preacher.

Also, just like most of the Amish family, Sam and his wife ended up having quite a few children. As Sam's children grew up, three of his own children left the community. Sam and his family lived in Ohio. Several years after we had moved to New York, Sam and his wife came to New York to visit. Sam had a brother that lived in New York, so I imagine that was one of the reasons why they had come to New York. Sam and his wife also stopped by our house to visit us while they were in New York. They even spend the night at our house.

While Sam and his wife were visiting, Sam mentioned to my father about his three children who had left the community. Sam was not very happy with his children leaving the community. From what it sounded like, Sam thought the outside life was a terrible place to live. He had told my father that he would rather see his children be buried in the cemetery than seeing them living the English life. Many may think this is a terrible thing to say about your own children, but the reason Sam would have rather seen his children in a cemetery than living in the outside world was that, the Amish believe once you leave the community, you will not make into heaven when your time comes. If Sam's children's time had come before they left, the Amish would believe they would make into heaven. But since they left the community, they no longer believe that.

The Amish do feel very bad when someone passes away, and they like to know that they will make it into heaven and God will take care of them. They don't feel that will happen when you leave the community, and this is why Sam said he would have rather seen his children in a cemetery than living the English life.

This one Amish man named Emmanuel Shelter was married to a woman named Barbara. Emmanuel and Barbara were living life, just like the rest of the Amish community. The time came where Emmanuel started to overstep the Amish rules, and every once in a while, the bishop would have a talk with him and tell him he could no longer keep doing that. One may wonder what would happen if a man or woman doesn't follow the rules or the religious. The time would come where the bishop would tell the person that they are no longer allowed in the community or to come to church, which is just what ended up happening for Emmanuel Shelter. The time came when Emmanuel was doing a lot of stuff that was not allowed in the community, and eventually, he was no longer accepted in the community.

Emmanuel had a well drilling business, and he was doing very well for himself. His well drilling machine was big enough that he would have to hire someone with a tractor to move it. The Amish community was perfectly fine with him hiring someone with a tractor to move his well drilling machine. In the Amish community, if you needed some kind of equipment to be moved that you are not able to do with horses, you are allowed to hire someone from the outside to have it moved for you.

When we had lived in Ohio, my father had started working with Emmanuel doing the well drilling. However, after Emmanuel started getting in trouble in the community, my father started to distance himself from him.

One of the first things Emmanuel did that was very against the Amish religion was buy a tractor. The reason Emmanuel decided to buy a tractor was so he didn't have to hire someone to move his well drilling machine. After the community found out that Emmanuel bought a tractor, that is when they no longer allow him in the community. Not being accepted in the community anymore doesn't mean that you have to find a new place to live; it just means that the Amish no longer look at you as one of them. They will look at you as an outsider.

Not long after Emmanuel bought a tractor, he decided to have an auction. The auction was to sell the stuff that he felt that he no longer had needs for. Emmanuel had gathered up quite a few things over the years, so he had a lot of stuff to sell. He also owned several different well drilling machines, and Emmanuel decided that he was going to sell all of his well drilling machines except for one of them he wanted to keep for himself.

For my father, he really enjoyed doing the well drilling and wanted to continue doing it, so when he heard Emmanuel was selling several of his well drilling machines, he was very interested in buying one of them, as he saw this as a good opportunity to have his own well drilling business. When the day of the auction came around, my father went to the auction. He even asked me and some of my brothers if we wanted to go as well. Of course, we wanted to go to the auction; going to auctions was one of our favorite things to do. It is not very often we would get to go to an auction, so when we did get the chance to go, we were very excited.

The day of Emmanuel's auction, there were a lot of Amish who had gathered together for his auction. I did not really watch what was being sold at the auction; I was pretty young at the time, and I was way more interested in playing games with some of the other children who had come to the auction with their parents. But I do remember it was in the afternoon getting towards evening, I happened to notice that the auctioneer and all the people who were following the auctioneer were getting close to where the well drilling machines were, and I had known it wouldn't be long before they would be selling them. So I went and stood where I could see the auctioneer and also where I could see my father, as I was very interested to see if my father was going to buy one of the well drillers.

Just as they started getting to where the well drillers were, I saw that my father was standing right next to the auctioneer. I was very excited to see my father stand right next to the auctioneer. I was hoping he would buy one of the well drillers. Sure enough, when they got to the one that my father was interested in buying, he ended up buying it. I was very excited, as I thought that was really something to watch my father buy a well drilling machine.

After that day, my father started his own well drilling business. Dan would often go with my father to help him with the well drilling, and

Dan enjoyed doing the well drilling a lot. For me, I only ever got to see my father using the well drilling machine a couple of times. One of those times was when he drilled a well for our neighbor, and the other time was when he drilled a well at our schoolhouse. At the time, I was too young to go with my dad to help with the well drilling, as I would not have been enough help for my father to take me with him.

I was always looking forward to the day when I could go with my dad and help him with the well drilling. However, that day never came. When we moved from Ohio to New York, my father decided to sell the well drilling machine, as he thought once we moved to New York, we would be too busy with other stuff that he would not have time to travel on the road well drilling. Instead of doing the well drilling after we had moved to New York, my father decided to buy a sawmill as that would bring in a fairly good income. We also had a lot of wooded land. My father decided we had plenty of wooded land that there had to be a way to make money from that. For the first couple of years, we didn't do much work in the woods other than cutting enough firewood for our heat during the winter time.

After a couple years of going in our woods and cutting firewood to heat our house, we noticed that we had quite a lot of maple trees. My father decided we had enough maple trees that he bought a maple evaporator. The evaporator was so we could collect the sap water from the tree and make maple syrup, and this would also help bring in income. I'm sure my mother was happy to see that we were able to make a living from home, and we didn't have to travel on the road to make ends meet. My mother always worried about when my father was traveling on the road, as she would hope everything would be going fine. The times where my mother would worry the most was when my father would not come home until late in the evening, as she worried something might have happened. Since we were not allowed to have phones, it wasn't like she could call my dad and make sure everything was okay. For my father, there were not too many times that he would come home late in the night. For the most part, he would try to be home by dark.

This was one thing Emmanuel Shelter would do quite often: come home late at night and leave early in the morning. After Emmanuel had bought a tractor, he no longer was traveling with a horse and buggy. When he would go to work or leave to go to town, Emmanuel was driving his tractor wherever he went. Barbara did not like that Emmanuel bought a tractor at all. But Emmanuel did not care what Barbara thought of what he was doing; he was simply going to do what he wanted to do. Barbara had said one time that she would often lay in bed at night and be very worried about where Emmanuel may be or if something may have happened to him.

One of the things that Emmanuel did to his tractor was figure out how to make his tractor go faster than it was supposed to. What he had done to it was not safe to be driving down the road, and when he would get to the top of a hill, he would put the tractor in neutral and let it roll down the hill, which was allowing him to go faster but also very dangerous.

Barbara had found out that this is what Emmanuel was doing, and she became even more worried. My father and some of the other Amish in the community were worried that the day would come where if Emmanuel kept doing what he was doing, he was going to have an accident, and it was going to be a bad accident. My father and several of the other Amish decided to go to Emmanuel's place and see if they could convince him not to drive the tractor anymore. They told Emmanuel that they were worried that "it is only going to be a matter of time until you have a bad accident."

However, Emmanuel didn't like to take advice from anybody and decided to keep doing what he was doing. It came to the point where we rarely heard from Emmanuel. We were getting into late summer/early fall when we had someone stop by our house early one morning to tell us that Emmanuel had a bad accident the day before, as it was later in the evening when the accident had happened. Emmanuel was driving down a road that not many people travel on, and nobody really lived in that area. By the time someone drove down that road and saw that there was an accident, it was already too late. Emmanuel didn't live to see another day.

It was an Amish person who had stopped by to tell us about Emmanuel's accident, but I do not remember who it was who stopped by. Many in the Amish community were very curious on how the accident had happened. From what we had heard, Emmanuel was going down the hill and was going way too fast for the tractor. As I'm not exactly sure what happened, all I remember hearing was that the tractor rolled over on top of Emmanuel. Emmanuel was able to make it out from under the tractor but was hurt way too much to walk somewhere and ask for help.

The Amish community gathered together to have a funeral for Emmanuel. I remember me and several of my siblings went to the wake, and my parents had also been there. I however did not go to the funeral. One of the things I remember was that they had the tractor that Emmanuel was driving parked close by the house, so everyone could easily see it. The reason for parking the tractor close to the house where everyone could see it was to show everyone what can happen when you do something that you are not supposed to do. The Amish thought that if Emmanuel didn't disobey the Amish religion, the accident would have never happened. The Amish have a very strong belief that once you get baptized and have made a commitment with God that you will follow the religion that you commit to, and if you break that commitment, God would no longer look out for you.

Emmanuel was breaking a lot of commitment that he had made to God. Not only was he breaking a lot of commitment from when he got baptized, he had also made a commitment to his wife when they got married to keep follow the Amish religion and take care of her "until death do us apart." Emmanuel did stay with his wife until he passed away, but you could say he was not doing a very good job at taking care of his wife and his children. For the last several years, Emmanuel did not follow the Amish religion or care what his wife thought.

The Amish feel when it is your time, it's your time no matter what you are doing. The question that often came to my mind was, would Emmanuel still be alive if he wasn't driving the tractor and would have kept obeying the Amish religion? Or was it simply his time no matter what he was doing? This is probably a question nobody will ever know.

In the Amish, when a couple is married and one of them passes away, they become a midwife or midman. If you do become a midwife or midman, you are allowed to get remarried if you wish to do so. For Barbara, she ended up getting remarried.

She was a midwife for quite a few years before she got remarried. Several years after we had moved to New York, we found out that Babara got remarried. One of our cousins who was living in Ohio had written us a letter to tell us that she got remarried. We were all happy to hear that she got remarried as we had hoped after everything she'd been through. She could finally enjoy living her life with her new husband.

CHAPTER TEN
AMISH ACCIDENTS

I F YOU DON'T LIKE READING ABOUT ACCIDENTS OR people getting hurt this may be one chapter you might want to skip.

In the Amish, there are quite a few accidents that happen. One of the accidents that you hear a lot is a buggy accident. When we had lived in Ohio, we would hear of buggy accidents all the time. A lot of the accidents were from a vehicle accidentally running into a buggy. Where we lived in Ohio was very hilly. It was easy for a vehicle coming up over top of a hill, and there would be a buggy just starting to go down the other side. Often the person driving the car would just simply not see the buggy and end up running into them. The amount of buggy accidents you heard of happening, you didn't hear that many of them got hurt very badly. Mostly just some bruises. Occasionally, you would hear of a very severe buggy accident.

Buggy accidents were not the only things that you would often hear. A lot of the Amish work with wood or are building something out of wood. Whenever they are building something, they use a table saw that is run by a gas power engine. If you are someone who uses a table saw a lot to cut lumber, it is easy to get very comfortable with getting your fingers very close to the table saw. Sometimes you get your fingers to close, which is just what happens for a lot of the Amish. One of Uncle

John's sons happens to be one of these people. He ended up getting his fingers too close to the saw blade and ended up losing three fingers. The Amish are very good with healing a lot of stuff when they get hurt. However, for something like this they would have to go to the hospital.

As for myself I also had my fair share of getting hurt. One of the first times I remember getting hurt really bad, or at least at the time I thought it was bad, happened one summer evening when I was seven years old.

During the summertime, we would eat supper at 5:00 and then after supper we would go out to do our evening chores. At the time, my job was to go out in the corn crib and fill three five gallons buckets, then take the buckets to the pig barn to feed the pigs. This evening, I was in a big hurry. Why I was in a big hurry, I have no idea. As soon as we got done eating supper, I took off running to the pig barn and got the five-gallon buckets, ran over to the corn crib. Our corn crib was built out of wood, and it had a wooden floor as well. The corn crib was getting to be an older corn crib. Some of the boards were getting pretty weak. One of the boards on the floor had gotten so weak, when I got up inside the corn crib the board broke and my foot went right through the floor.

The corn crib got built about two feet from the ground. Over the years, underneath the crib got used for storage for old barn boards. One of the boards had nails in it. During the summer time it was rare that we would wear shoes. For the most part, we would be barefooted. When my foot went through the floor, I had nothing protecting my foot. My foot ended up stepping right on the boards with the nails in it, and one of the nails went right through my foot. When I realized that I had a nail in my foot I took my other foot and stepped on the board to hold the board down so I could pull the nail out of my foot by just lifting my leg up. After I got the nail pulled out of my foot, I took off running to the house. As I was running to the house I was also crying.

When I got to the house, I told my mother what had happened. My mother put some kind of salve on it and then wrapped it up. After my mother wrapped it up, she told me to go lay in bed and rest for a while. I didn't end up going back out in the barn to help with the chores that evening. Instead, I stayed in bed until the next morning. For something like this, we did not go to the hospital. Once a day, my mother would take off the wrap and clean the foot, then put salve on it and wrap it back up. We did this until the foot was healed.

This was not the only time I got hurt. Shortly after I turned the age of 10 years old, I got hurt again. It was again during the summer. It was a very beautiful day. Me and my brothers were putting hay in the barn. In the Amish, the way we put hay in the barn, we had a hay mover that we cut our hay with. After several days of letting the hay dry, we would take our hay rake and rake the hay into rows, which were called hay rows. After our hay was all raked into rows, it was ready to be put in the barn. All of our hay had to be put in the barn loose because using a hay bailer was not allowed in the Amish community. Putting the hay in the barn loose was not all that hard either. We had what was called a hay loader that went behind the wagon. A team of horses were hooked to the wagon, and the hay loader was hooked behind the wagon. As you were going down through the field, you drove right over top of the hay rows and the hay loader that was hooked behind the wagon would pick up the hay and bring it up onto the wagon. We were actually able to put in quite a lot of hay in a day.

As for how I got hurt, every time the wagon would fill up, we had to unhook the hay loader from the wagon and take the wagon load of hay to the barn and unload it. When we got back to the field, we hooked the hay loader back to the wagon again. One of us would have to jump off the wagon and hook the hay loader to the wagon while the wagon was back up to the loader. That day, jumping off the wagon and hooking the loader to the wagon was my job. As for this time, I was simply not paying enough attention. As the wagon was backing up to the hay loader, I picked up the hay loader tongue to hook to the wagon. On the back end of the wagon, there was a hook where the hay loader hooked to. I ended up getting one of my fingers right between the end of the hay loader tongue and the wagon hook. My finger got smashed up very badly. As soon as my finger got hurt, I instantly felt very bad pain. As soon as I felt the pain, I took my other hand and wrapped it around my finger. I started screaming and crying as it had felt like I just lost my finger.

My brother Dan was the one on the wagon backing up to the loader. When Dan realized that I had hurt my finger, he came jumping off the wagon and wanted to see my finger to see how bad it really was. I showed my finger to Dan. My finger was smashed up so bad that Dan was not even able to look at my finger. Dan told me that I needed to go to the house and have our mother warp up my finger. So I took off running to the house. Luckily the house had not been that far away.

When I got to the house, I started looking for my mother. I didn't end up finding her in the house. Instead I found her in the wash house. The wash house was built off the side of our house and was used for doing all of our laundry and was also used for cleaning and canning a lot of our vegetables. When I got to the wash house and saw that my mother was in the wash house, I sat down by the doorway and was still crying. My mother came and looked at my finger and was very surprised by how bad my finger was smashed. My mother went into the house to get stuff to wrap up my finger. Meanwhile, I was feeling so much pain that I ended up having to lay down on the floor. I lay there until my mother wrapped up my finger.

When my mother got done wrapping up my finger, she told me that we might have to go to the hospital and have stitches put in my finger. My father had left early that day to go to town and was not going to be home until later that afternoon. My mother told me when my father got home, he'd have to look at it and see whether we had to go to the hospital or not. I went and lay in bed until my father got home.

My father got back home around 4:00 that afternoon. My mother told my father what had happened, and my father came and took the wrap of my finger so he could see how bad it really was. My father only looked at my finger for a few seconds and said, "We will definitely have to go to the hospital and have stitches put in your finger."

The hospital that we went to was around 13 miles away. To travel 13 miles with a horse and buggy where we had lived in Ohio would have taken all of an hour and a half and maybe even more because of being so hilly, so my father decided to go to one of our English neighbors and ask them if they would have time to take me and my father to the hospital. When he came back home, he said that the neighbor would be able to take us to the hospital and they would be over shortly. I started to get worried that I might get sick going for a car ride, as this was going to be the first time I went for a car ride that I could remember. Going to ask our neighbor to take us somewhere was only allowed if it was because of an accident; otherwise, we have to travel by horse and buggy or by a bus.

The reason I was worried that I would get sick going for a car ride was because I had often heard that if you don't rarely ever go for a car ride, it is very easy to get sick, and this was just the case for a lot of the Amish. At the time, one of my friends from school was in my grade. I had remembered that he said he went for a car ride and ended up getting car sick really bad. Luckily for me going to the hospital and coming back home, the car ride never bothered me. On our way to the hospital, I was in pain bad enough where it most likely kept my mind off the car ride. But for the ride back home, I was not nearly in as much pain. The doctor did a very good job fixing my finger. I ended up having 10 stitches put in my finger.

Going to the hospital was something that I had never experienced before. It was an eye opener for me to see a hospital, as we never really got to go that far outside the community. When we got to the hospital, we went inside and waited for a while until a doctor came by and called for us to follow him into one of the rooms where they ended up working on my finger. After we got into the room, we sat there for some time until another doctor came into the room. This doctor was an older man, and his name was Wayne. Wayne was the doctor who ended up working on my finger. Before Wayne came into the room, every once in a while I could hear people screaming very loud, and the screaming sounding like it was mostly young children. I thought to myself, *They must be screaming because the doctor is working on them, and it is very painful.* As I was thinking that, *When the doctor works on me I'm not going to scream even if it is painful,* as I didn't want anyone to hear me. I thought it would make me look weak.

When Dr. Wayne came into the room, he asked us some questions, which I pretty well was not able to answer any questions as I simply didn't understand most of the questions that he asked. Thankfully my father was there, and he was able to answer all his questions. When Dr. Wayne got done asking the question that he wanted to know, he then started to take the wrap off my finger. After he had taken the wrap off my finger, he took water and washed my finger. When he got done washing my finger, he had to numb my finger, so I wouldn't feel any pain when he worked on my finger. The numbing of my finger was more painful than when he was fixing up my finger. When Dr. Wayne started numbing my finger, he told me to scream as loud as I could, so I did.

At the time, I couldn't figure out why he wanted me to scream as loud as I could. It wasn't until sometime later it came to my mind why he had me scream so loud. For Dr. Wayne to have me scream as loud as I could was going to take my mind off from feeling the pain when he was numbing my finger. I also remember lying there and watching Dr. Wayne stitch up my finger. As I got older, I often wondered how I was able to watch the doctor put stitches in my finger. There is certainly no way that I would be able to do that now.

After the doctor had my finger all fixed up, he told me to not do much for work several weeks. In the Amish, when we get hurt like this and are supposed to take it easy until we are healed up, it doesn't mean that we are not going to work. It is most likely that we will do something that is considered "easy" work. For me, I was back out working within a couple of days. One of the things I remember doing was picking cherries. We had three different cherries: two of the cherry trees were sour cherry trees; the other cherry tree was a black cherry tree. The black cherry tree was a very big cherry tree and produced a lot of cherries. I'm not exactly sure how many cherries we got from the black cherry tree, but I do remember we would can well over 100 quarts of cherries a year. We would have some kind of fruit every meal, and the black cherries were one of the fruits we would often eat. For the sour cherry, we would use them to make pies. Pretty well all of our cherries were canned and then opened as needed. It just so happened that it was prime cherry picking season when I hurt my finger. My father asked me if I thought picking cherries was something I could do. Picking cherries was something I had always enjoyed doing. So of course, I told my father I thought that I could pick cherries.

Our cherry trees were pretty tall, we would have to use a very tall ladder to pick the cherries. Either one of my brothers or my father would stand a ladder up in the tree, so I could climb up the ladder and pick cherries. Whenever I needed it to be moved, someone would move it for me. Picking cherries was not very hard work. I took a gallon bucket and hung it onto the ladder, and when the bucket was close to being full, I would take it down the ladder and dump the cherries in a different container and go back up the ladder and keep picking cherries.

As the time came, my finger was all healed back up and I didn't have to take it easy anymore. I'm not certain how long my finger was wrapped up until the day came where we went to the doctor to have my finger unwrapped and had the stitches taken out. I would say it was not more than four weeks that my finger was wrapped up. We didn't have to go back to the hospital to have my stitches taken out. Instead, we were able to go to a different place that was only around five miles from our place, and we were able to drive there by horse and buggy.

If I remember right, the doctor we went to was a private doctor. I could never remember this doctor's name. When he took the stitches out of my finger, he took the stitches and put them on a small piece of wood and told me that it was mine to take home and keep. He said this will be something for you to always remember. But of course, my father wouldn't let me keep the piece of wood with the stitches.

After that day, I never saw that piece of wood again. There were only two things that I could think that my father did with the piece of wood. One would be to hide somewhere where he knew I would never find it. The second thing would have been to burn it. After I had left the community, I ended up reaching out to this doctor. The reason for reaching out to him was because I was trying to get my passport. At the time, I lived close to Canada, and I had known some people who would occasionally go there. Just the thought of being able to go to a different country would be very cool to experience. In order to do so, I was going to need a passport. Getting a passport, I needed to be able to come up with as much information about me and my family as I could. But since the Amish don't have any identification of themselves, it is pretty impossible to show any proof of who your family is, and it was not like I was going to get any help from my family. Luckily, by this time I got to know Mark and Loraine very well. Loraine was a very smart person and was helping with getting my passport. It came to the point where she thought that I was not going to be able to get my passport simply because I couldn't show enough proof who I was, and who my family was. Loriane was telling me some of the things that I would need in order to get my passport, and one of the things she said that would be a big help is that if I ever was to a doctor and could show proof of that. I told Loriane that I was to the hospital when I was young but didn't have anything to show that I was at the hospital. I also told Loriane that I went to a different place to have my stitches taken out, and I still remembered what town that was in, which was Mt. Hope, Ohio. So Loriane decided to see if she could reach out to that doctor and see if he had any information about me that could be helpful. She was able to reach out to the doctor. The doctor seemed to know my parents very well. I was very surprised by that; I had no idea that he had known my parents that well. I had often wondered how he had known my parents that well, but the only way I could figure was my parents went to him when they had us children.

It just so happened that I was at Mark and Loriane's place when she reached out to the doctor. I ended up also speaking to the doctor. Not only was I surprised by how well he knew my parents, but he was also able to speak Pennsylvania Dutch very well. While I was talking on the phone with him, he asked me questions, such as what I was doing for work and how I liked living outside life. He also told me that he was retired from his job, and he and his wife had bought a camper, and they were doing a lot of traveling. He said he thought maybe someday they would make it to New York. Before I got done speaking to him, he told me that he thought he would probably have plenty of information about me and my family, and I would be able to get my passport. He said he would send the information to us in the mail.

It turned out to be just like he thought, the information was plenty of information for me to get my passport. Being he had known my parents so well, I was surprised by how open and willing he was to want to help me, and he had also wished me the best of luck on my journey. I was very thankful for his help.

CHAPTER ELEVEN
EXPERIENCING A DIFFERENT AMISH RELIGION

THERE ARE MANY DIFFERENT AMISH RELIGIONS, but the Old Order Amish was the only other Amish religion that I got to experiencing. When I left the Amish community the first time, my plan was to return to the Amish when I got the age of 21. Instead of returning to the Amish when I turned 21, I ended up moving from New York to Indiana. My oldest brother Harvey lived in Indiana and had his own construction company. Harvey offered for me to come work for him. At the time, I was not making much money where I was working, and the offer that he gave me was good enough that I thought I couldn't turn it down. Two days after I turned 21, I moved to Indiana.

Harvey had also left the Amish when he was 17. After he had left, he got to know a lot of the Old Order Amish. The Old Order Amish are very different from the Swartzentruber Amish. The Old Order Amish are allowed to do a lot more than the Swartzentruber Amish. Being that Harvey was around the Old Order a lot after he had left, the time came where he liked the Old Order Amish enough that he decided to join their religion.

If you are someone who leaves the Amish before you get baptized the Old Order doesn't hold anything against you if you do leave the Amish. For someone like me leaving and not being baptized, the Old

Order would allow me to work with them if I wanted to. When I moved to Indiana, Harvey was living with an older couple. Their names are Maynard and Vera.

Maynard and Vera were living in a pretty big house at the time. They only had one son who was still living at home. The rest of their children were married and had their own place. Maynard and Vera also offered me to stay with them till I found a place on my own. I was very surprised that Maynard and Vera offered to stay with them because I was living the English life. I was very amazed by how different the Old Order Amish were versus the Swartzentruber. For the Old Order, when their children turn the age of 16 years old, they are allowed to experience the English life and still live at home. They are allowed to buy a vehicle and get their driver's license and be able to drive. They could have a cell phone; they were allowed to park their vehicle at home, and the parents were perfectly fine with their children doing that. They could live this kind of lifestyle until they decided to get baptized and join the church. Once they joined the church, they had to follow the religion.

For their children, when they turned 16 and wanted to get a cell phone and buy a car, they were pretty well on their own to do so, except for this one family. Their son worked for Harvey for part of a summer, and he was right around the age of 16, and the word was going around that when he wanted to buy a car. His parents ended up buying a car for him. Some of the Amish thought that the parents may have gone a little too far to buy their son a car. The reason was because it almost made it look like they wanted their son to live the English life instead of the Amish. However, it was not against the Old Order religious to buy their children a car once they turned 16, especially not in the area I was living.

While I was living at Maynard's, there were several different times where I was asked if I would want to eventually join their church. Of course, at first I did not have an answer. I ended up staying at Maynard's for about six months, which was much longer than I thought I would. The reason I had stayed with them for six months before I found a place of my own was because, at the time, we were working anywhere from three to six hours away from home. Working that far away from home, we ended up staying at a hotel during the week and then traveled home for the weekend. I moved to Indiana in the fall and most of that winter we worked on the road. When spring came, we started getting busy enough working around home, where we did not have to travel far away to work. Since I was able to be home every night, I thought it would be best if I got a place on my own and no longer had to live at Maynard's. It was not that I wasn't enjoying living at Maynard's. I had actually enjoyed living at Maynard's very much, I liked the feeling of being around the Amish life, but since I was not one of Maynard's children and I was not living the Amish life, I thought it would be best if I got a place on my own, which is just what I ended up doing. I hoped that Maynard didn't feel like I was taking advantage of them for staying there for so long.

I only lived in Indiana for two years before I ended up moving back to New York. During the two years I lived in Indiana, I learned a lot and got to do things that I had always wanted to do. One of the things I got to do was fly in an airplane. This was one thing that was on the top of my to do list ever since I had left. After close to a year living in Indiana, I decided to go back to New York to visit my friends. Instead of driving, I decided I wanted to fly. From my place to the airport was a three-hour drive, and it was a very snowy day. The roads were covered with snow and slush, making it very hard to drive.

While I was driving down the interstate, I saw a lot of cars going off the road into the digs. The amount of cars I saw going off the road, I was worried that I might come up on an accident where the road would be closed, and I wouldn't make it to the airport in time. Luckily, I made it to the airport on time. When I got to the airport, I started looking for parking signs where I could park my vehicle for the week.

I was able to find the parking area very easily. Once I parked, I got my bag and went into the airport. When I got inside and started looking to see where I needed to go, I was very surprised how big the place was. I had never been inside a building this big; not even close. My first thought was, *I hope I don't get lost in this place and have no idea where to go.* There ended up being plenty of signs that I could follow, and it brought me where I needed to be. I ended up making plenty of time. Now I was sitting there, waiting till it was time to go onto the plane. After about half an hour sitting there waiting, it was finally time to go onto the plane.

As I started going onto the plane, my heart started beating a little faster, as I was getting a little nervous. I started thinking, *What if we end up having an accident and the plane crashes, and that will be the end of my life?* But then I told myself I can't think that way; I have to go with the flow and enjoy the moment.

The plane was very hot until we were almost ready to take off. I was also not the only one who was very warm. I heard many others talk about how warm it was. Before we took off, I felt that they turned the heat way down, and it became much more comfortable.

I found the plane ride to be very fun and exciting. I couldn't wait to fly back home. The airport I went to was Detroit Michigan, and I flew to Burlington, Vermont, and had one of my friends pick me up from there. When it was time to go back home, he brought me back to the airport.

After I got back home, it was time to go back to normal life and go to work. As I continued working for my brother and as everyday went by, I got to know more about the Old Order religion. One thing I was hoping I would get to do sometime was go to their church. The day came where the church was at Maynard's place, and they invited me to come to the church. In order for me to go to their church, I had to wear Amish clothes. I didn't mind having to wear Amish clothes to go to their church, as I was very interested in seeing how their church was compared to our church when I was living at home.

It turned out that the Old Order was very similar to the Swartzentruber church. There were several things that were done differently. One of the things was what the preacher was preaching. In the Swartzentruber church, the preacher would only preach things that were written in the Bible. In the Old Order church, there was not a lot of preaching from the Bible. Instead, the preacher preaches mostly about things that he experiences during his life, or if something has happened to someone that he knew or had heard about, he would preach about that, like for example, if someone had left Amish and something bad had happened to him, such as having a bad accident, and after the accident the person returned to the Amish and ended up joining the church and getting married. Those are the things that I noticed the Old Order would preach about.

However, if there was someone who had left the Amish and was doing very well living the English life, that was something they would not preach about. The reason that they would not preach about that is because they don't want their children knowing that the English can be a great life to live, as they may be worried if they talk good about the English life that their children may want to live the English life instead of the Amish. For the Old Order, they certainly didn't talk as bad about the English life as Swartzentruber did.

And they certainly didn't tell their children if they left the Amish that no one in the community would ever forgive them for what they had done, that even God wouldn't be able to forgive you for what you did, and when your time comes, instead of making it in heaven He would make a hot fire and burn your body. One of the reasons that I had wanted to go to the Old Order Amish church was because I wanted to see if there is anything in the Bible or if the preacher was going to preach what would happen for someone like me. But the times that I went, the preacher never preached anything about that. I was very curious for quite some time and decided to look into getting a Bible and reading it myself. The only Bible I could find was written in

English, but I was always used to reading a Bible in German. Reading the Eible in English just didn't seem the same to me, so I never ended up getting a Bible, as I thought to myself, *I will probably live the rest of my life not knowing.*

I also got the opportunity to go to one of the Old Order Amish weddings. I had always wanted to go to one of their weddings. This wasn't going to be the first time that I went to an Old Order wedding, but it was going to be the first time I would be old enough to remember how it was done. When we still lived in Ohio, I was only the age of four years old. One of our neighbors who was Old Order did have a wedding, and they invited our family. If I remember, it was only me and my fatherwho went to the wedding. For my mother, it wouldn't have interested her to go to a wedding that wasn't the same religion as we were. A lot of people who don't know much about the Amish, they hear the words "Old Order Amish" and think because of the name, "Old Order Amish," that they must be very strict. Instead, it is quite the opposite. My mother not going was not going to stop my father from going to their wedding if he was invited, as he was interested to see how their weddings are compared to ours.

But for me being so young, I barely remember anything about the wedding. About the only things I do remember are, in the afternoon when everyone was sitting around the tables and singing, they passed around the bowl of candy bars, and I was able to get a candy bar. That is pretty much all I remember about the wedding. So when I got the opportunity to go to an Old Order Amish wedding after I had moved to Indiana, I was very excited. The wedding I got to go to was for my brother Harvey. There were certainly things that were done differently from what I was used to.

For Harvey to get married in a different Amish religion was something our parents didn't approve of. Harvey was aware that our parents would not approve and probably would not come to the wedding, but Harvey decided to invite them anyhow as he thought that would be the right thing to do. Just like Harvey thought, they never showed up for his wedding.

The one thing I found being a lot different was, in the Swartzentruber weddings, only the women would be table waiters, and in the Old Orders, for every girl who was a table waiter, there was a guy. I ended up having to be a waiter. By the end of the day, I had decided being a waiter was certainly one of my least favorite things to do. The Old Order Amish wedding also isn't as long as the Swartzentruber is. For the Old Order, their weddings are usually done by 7:00 or 8:00 in the evening.

Once I got to know the Old Order religion somewhat, I could see why their children would choose the Amish life over the English. The Old Orders have a very peaceful living. As far as all the places that I had lived and the different lives that I got to experience and all the people I got to know, the Old Order Amish have by far the most peaceful living life. There were many times that I thought of joining their church, and several different times, I had actually thought I was going to join their church.

The one thing that was holding me back from doing so was my brother Harvey. After I started working for Harvey, the time came where we didn't really see eye to eye. Harvey wasn't afraid to tell the community just what he thought of me. Most of the things that he thought of me were not good. Being that I was a new person in the community and Harvey had all negative things to say about me, I didn't make many friends. You could say I didn't make any friends at all. Instead of being able to make friends, everyone seemed to mostly look down on who I was. The time came where I knew if I was going to join their church, I would not be able to enjoy my life. It was certainly disappointing, knowing that joining the Old Order church was something I was not going to be able to do and feel like I could fit in. As much as I had always wanted to live the Amish life and enjoy that lifestyle, once again, it seemed like everything was against me to do so.

I had often thought if I would have moved to Indiana and it wasn't to work for my brother, it is most likely I would have joined the Old Order religion. However, if everything was against me, to do it was probably not meant to be.

The other thing the Old Order did that we didn't do at home and I don't think we would have been allowed to do, as it would have been again our religion, was when it was a holiday, the families would all gather together for a mid-morning brunch. This would mostly happen at Thanksgiving and Christmas.

When Maynard or one of their children had holiday brunch at their place, they would always invite me, and for the most part, I would go, as there was not much else for me to do other than stay at home and be bored. I had always enjoyed the holiday brunch. There was lots of great food, and you got to hear what everyone was doing and how their life was going.

There was usually a lot of singing and playing games. One of the games that would often be played was "corn hole." Most of the day was usually very interesting. One of the things the Old Order would talk a lot about, that you didn't hear that much in the Swartzentruber relion, was how nice their horses looked or who had the best-looking horse. The Old Order certainly had some very nice-looking horses, and some were very expensive. Some of the horses would look just like show horses, almost too nice looking to drive down the road. For some, I think they looked at it as competition to who could have the nieces looking horse.

For the Swartzentruber gathering together and having a holiday brunch, talking about who had the nicest horse would have been considered too high class. We had one time this family that came to visit us one Sunday. While they were visiting, they mentioned that they were thinking of having a homecoming where all their children would come home to visit them on a Sunday. That evening after the family had gone home my father said he was surprised they were considering having a homecoming. My father said a homecoming was against our religion. They had a very big family, the biggest Amish family I had ever heard of. The family had 20 or 21 one boys and three or four girls. With all their children it, added up to be in the mid-twenties. As for the homecoming, I'm not certain if it ever happened.

The Old Order also had some very nice lighting in their houses. Their lights were propane lights. In the evening before we went to bed, we would sit around and read a newspaper or a book. There was not really anything else to do before bed time to keep us entertained. With the propane lights, you see much better when you are reading. A lot better than the oil lamps that we had at home.

In the Amish, there is this newspaper that you get every week, and the newspaper is something that I believe only the Amish get it, and I think it was only the Swartzentruber that would get it since I don't ever remember from seeing this newspaper at an Old Order's home. The paper was called *Budget*. Why was it call *Budget*? I have no idea. The newspaper had nothing to do with what the word actually means. The way *Budget* would work is, in almost every community, there was one Amish person who would write several different paragraphs. They would mostly write about what was going on in the community, such as how the weather was doing, who had the church and who was going to have the church, or if someone got married. So when we got *Budget*, we would always read what other communities were doing.

As for the lighting, I'm not certain what kind of lighting the Old Orders used in their barns, but I do know for some they had electric lights hooked up in their barns and would run a generator for their lights. This may have been one of those things where they were right on the edge of going against their religion.

The day came where I realized my time living in Indiana was coming to an end, as I simply did not enjoy my life enough to stay in Indiana. I thought of my friends a lot back in New York and had known they would be glad to see me moving back, which is what I ended up doing. There were quite a few things that did not get to do while I was living in Indiana. I enjoyed going skiing, and living in Indiana, I did not get to do this. At the time, going skiing was something I craved. Several years after I had moved back, me and one of the guys I was working with went cross country skiing two days before Halloween. It was the first time I went cross country skiing. We went to White Face Mountain; the top of the mountain is right close to 5,000 feet elevation. We cross country skied all the way to the top. It was about three and half miles one way. We made it up and back down in four hours. I was very tired when I got home. My legs felt like Jell-O.

In Indiana, it was not that we didn't get enough snow; it was because the land was very flat, and there were no hills for miles. I waited to move back to New York until late fall. During the summertime was a very busy time for my brother, and I didn't want to just up and leave during the busy time. I did tell him once we got into late fall, I was planning on moving back to New York. During the time when I told Harvey that I was going to move back to New York, he had three other workers plus a few part timers. My thought was with all those workers, if I left in late fall, he would be able to fill my spot by spring time.

Things didn't turn out quite like I thought they would. About three weeks before I had planned to move to New York, all of the other workers quit working for him. Now I started having a second thought about moving back to New York, as this was not the way I had wanted it to end. But I had already told my landlord that I would be moving out and someone else had planned to rent the place the following month. So I was kind of up against the wall not knowing what to do. I did a lot of thinking for a few days and decided I was going to continue with my plan and move to New York. I felt bad leaving like this but hoped Harvey would find workers to replace me and the other workers who quit. I worked for Harvey until the last week in October. My last day was on Friday, and the next morning was when I was moving back to New York, as it was getting close to the end of October.

Every night after I got home from work, I would work on packing up my stuff, so when Saturday morning came, I was going to be ready to go. At the time, I was driving a car, and there was no way I was going to be able to fit everything in my car. One of my friends in New York and his family were farmers and had several different trailers, so I decided to call him and see if he would want to drive to Indiana to pick all my stuff up and bring it back to New York. I had second thoughts before I called him, thinking that he probably would not want to drive that far. It was all of an 11-hour drive. He didn't think twice; he said he would have no problem coming to move me back to New York.

He showed up around 6:00 on Friday evening, and we loaded up pretty much all my stuff that evening. We wanted to be able to leave early the next morning. The trailer that he brought was an enclosed trailer, and it was pretty big even after we put all my furniture in there. There was still plenty of room in the trailer, so we decided to put my car in the trailer, and we could ride back together.

We got up earlier the next morning. I still had a few things to put in the trailer and then we left. We left early enough that we drove for a couple of hours until it started to get daylight. Once we started heading to New York, I started to get very excited, as I was looking forward to spending time with my friends.

We arrived at our destination around 4:00 that afternoon, which was in Bangor, New York. I may do my fair share of moving around, but Bangor, New York, is always where I call home.